Tucholsky Wagner Zola Scott Sydow Fonatne Schlegel Freud
Turgenev Wallace
Twain Walther von der Vogelweide Fouqué Friedrich II. von Preußen
Weber Freiligrath Frey
Fechner Fichte Weiße Rose von Fallersleben Kant Ernst Richthofen Frommel
Hölderlin
Fehrs Engels Fielding Eichendorff Tacitus Dumas
Faber Flaubert
Feuerbach Maximilian I. von Habsburg Fock Eliasberg Zweig Ebner Eschenbach
Ewald Eliot Vergil
Goethe London
Mendelssohn Balzac Shakespeare Elisabeth von Österreich
Lichtenberg Rathenau Dostojewski Ganghofer
Trackl Stevenson Tolstoi Hambruch Doyle Gjellerup
Mommsen Thoma Lenz Hanrieder Droste-Hülshoff
Dach Verne von Arnim Hägele Hauff Humboldt
Reuter
Karrillon Garschin Rousseau Hagen Hauptmann Gautier
Damaschke Defoe Hebbel Baudelaire
Descartes
Wolfram von Eschenbach Schopenhauer Hegel Kussmaul Herder
Bronner Darwin Melville Dickens Grimm Jerome Rilke George
Campe Horváth Aristoteles Bebel Proust
Bismarck Vigny Gengenbach Barlach Voltaire Federer Herodot
Heine
Storm Casanova Lessing Tersteegen Gilm Grillparzer Georgy
Chamberlain Langbein Gryphius
Brentano Lafontaine
Strachwitz Claudius Schiller Kralik Iffland Sokrates
Katharina II. von Rußland Bellamy Schilling
Gerstäcker Raabe Gibbon Tschechow
Löns Hesse Hoffmann Gogol Wilde Gleim Vulpius
Luther Heym Hofmannsthal Morgenstern
Roth Heyse Klopstock Klee Hölty Kleist Goedicke
Luxemburg Puschkin Homer Mörike
La Roche Horaz Musil
Machiavelli Kierkegaard Kraft Kraus
Navarra Aurel Musset
Nestroy Marie de France Lamprecht Kind Kirchhoff Hugo Moltke
Nietzsche Nansen Laotse Ipsen Liebknecht
Marx Ringelnatz
von Ossietzky Lassalle Gorki Klett Leibniz
May vom Stein Lawrence Irving
Petalozzi Platon Knigge
Sachs Pückler Michelangelo Kafka
Poe Liebermann Kock
de Sade Praetorius Mistral Zetkin Korolenko

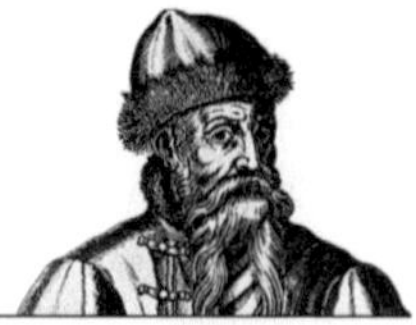

The publishing house tredition has created the series **TREDITION CLASSICS.** It contains classical literature works from over two thousand years. Most of these titles have been out of print and off the bookstore shelves for decades.

The book series is intended to preserve the cultural legacy and to promote the timeless works of classical literature. As a reader of a **TREDITION CLASSICS** book, the reader supports the mission to save many of the amazing works of world literature from oblivion.

The symbol of **TREDITION CLASSICS** is Johannes Gutenberg (1400 – 1468), the inventor of movable type printing.

With the series, tredition intends to make thousands of international literature classics available in printed format again – worldwide.

All books are available at book retailers worldwide in paperback and in hard-cover. For more information please visit: www.tredition.com

tredition®

tredition was established in 2006 by Sandra Latusseck and Soenke Schulz. Based in Hamburg, Germany, tredition offers publishing solutions to authors and publishing houses, combined with worldwide distribution of printed and digital book content. tredition is uniquely positioned to enable authors and publishing houses to create books on their own terms and without conventional manufacturing risks.

For more information please visit: www.tredition.com

Memoirs of Journeys to Venice and the Low Countries

Albrecht Dürer

Imprint

This book is part of the TREDITION CLASSICS series.

Author: Albrecht Dürer
Cover design: toepferschumann, Berlin (Germany)

Publisher: tredition GmbH, Hamburg (Germany)
ISBN: 978-3-8491-8510-7

www.tredition.com
www.tredition.de

TABLE OF CONTENTS

BASIC BACKGROUND

Albrecht Dürer (1471-1528) was probably the greatest graphical artist of the Northern Renaissance. He is the first to have elevated the self-portrait to a high art form, and was known for his fascination with animals, which form the subjects of many of his graphical works. He reveled in portraying men of learning and/or high stature as well as peasants, believing that portraits of the latter could be as instructive as those of the former. His marriage to his wife Agnes was childless and banal, apparently because Dürer was too preoccupied with intellectual matters to be much interested in romantic pursuits.

In the letters below, this unusually modern thinker demonstrates his noble, righteous utilitarian personal philosophy, and meticulously records his personal and travel expenses, while journeying throughout Venice and various other European cities and divided German states. Numerous kings and laypeople sought to meet and host him, since he was renowned and loved as a painter while still alive. He comments on Martin Luther, Erasmus of Rotterdam and painting, and demonstrates his curious, inquiring nature. He also describes his visit to Zeeland to see a beached whale, which washed away before he got there; but during this visit, Dürer may have caught the disease from which he may have died several years later. Like Rembrandt, he enjoyed collecting things, and demonstrates this in his letters.

****

BRIEF EXCERPT FROM THE INTRODUCTION TO THE 1913 EDITION, WRITTEN BY ROGER FRY (1866-1934):

Whatever one's final estimate of his art, Dürer's personality is at once so imposing and so attractive, and has been so endeared to us by familiarity, that something of this personal attachment has been transferred to our aesthetic judgment. The letters from Venice and the Diary of his journey in the Netherlands, which form the contents of this volume, are indeed the singularly fortunate means for this pleasant intercourse with the man himself. They reveal Dürer as one of the distinctively modern men of the Renaissance: intensely, but not arrogantly, conscious of his own personality; accepting with a pleasant ease the universal admiration of his genius-a personal admiration, too, of an altogether modern kind; careful of his fame as one who foresaw its immortality. They show him as having, though in a far less degree, something of Leonardo da Vinci's scientific interest, certainly as possessing a quick, though naive curiosity about the world and a quite modern freedom from superstition. It is clear that his dominating and yet kindly personality, no less than his physical beauty and distinction, made him the center of interest wherever he went. His easy and humorous good- fellowship, of which the letters to Pirkheimer are eloquent, won for him the admiring friendship of the best men of his time.

To all these characteristics we must add a deep and sincere religious feeling, which led him to side with the leaders of the Reformation, a feeling which comes out in his passionate sense of loss when he thinks that Luther is about to be put to death, and causes him to write a stirring letter to Erasmus, urging him to continue the work of reform. For all that, there is no trace in him of either Protestantism or Puritanism. He was perhaps fortunate—certainly as an artist he was fortunate—to live at a time when the line of cleavage between the reformers and the Church was not yet so marked as to compel a decisive action.

****

CAST OF [SOME OF THE] CHARACTERS:

Agnes: Dürer's wife
Wilibald Pirkheimer: Dürer's best friend
Wolgemut: The master painter to whom Dürer began formal training as an apprentice. Later, Dürer painted a richly detailed self-portrait of him.
Giovanni Bellini: Famous Renaissance painter and contemporary of Dürer.
Jan van Eyk: Famous Renaissance painter.
Imhof: Hans Imhof, the elder, at Nuremberg; the younger Imhof was in Venice.
Schott: Kunz Schott, an enemy of the town of Nuremberg.
Weisweber: A Nuremberg general.

****

FORMS OF MONEY REFERRED TO IN THE LETTERS:

Marcelli: A Venetian coin worth 10 soldi.
Stiver: A Netherlandish coin worth about 80 pfennigs.
Philip's: A Netherlandish coin worth rather less than a Rhenish florin.
Crown: A Netherlandish coin worth 6.35 marks.
Noble: The Rosennobel = 8 marks, 20 pfennigs. The Flemish noble = 9 marks, 90 pfennigs.
Blanke: A silver coin = 2 stivers.
Angel: An English coin = 2 florins, 2 stivers Netherlandish.

****

PART 1: LETTERS FROM VENICE TO WILIBALD PIRKHEIMER

Venice, 6th January, 1506

To the Honourable and wise Wilibald Pirkheimer, in Nuremberg.

My dear Master, To you and all yours, many happy good New Years. My willing service to you, dear Herr Pirkheimer. Know that I am in good health; may God send you better even than that. Now as to what you commissioned me, namely, to buy a few pearls and precious stones, you must know that I can find nothing good enough or worth the money: everything is snapped up by the Germans.

Those who go about on the Riva always expect four times the value for anything, for they are the falsest knaves that live there. No one expects to get an honest service of them. For that reason some good people warned me to be on my guard against them. They told me that they cheat both man and beast, and that you could buy better things for less money at Frankfort than at Venice.

As for the books which I was to order for you, Imhof has already seen to it, but if you are in need of anything else, let me know, and I shall do it for you with all zeal. And would to God that I could do you some real good service. I should gladly accomplish it, since I know how much you do for me.

And I beg of you be patient with my debt, for I think oftener of it than you do. As soon as God helps me to get home I will pay you honourably, with many thanks; for I have to paint a picture for the Germans, for which they are giving me 110 Rhenish gulden, which will not cost me as much as five. I shall have finished laying and scraping the ground-work in eight days, then I shall at once begin to paint, and if God will, it shall be in its place for the altar a month after Easter.

[Editor note: This refers to the [altarpiece called the] "Madonna of the Rose Garlands," painted for the chapel of S. Bartolommeo, the burial-place of the German colony. About the year 1600 it was bought for a high price by the Emperor Rudolf II, who is said to have had it carried [over the Alps] by four men all the way to Prague to avoid the risk of damage in transport. [It suffered serious water damage during the Thirty Years' War of 1618-1648, and many parts of it had to be repainted to replace much of the original paint that was lost, but] it still remains one of the most important [and lavishly colored] of all Dürer's works.]

The money I hope, if God will, to put by; and from that I will pay you: for I think that I need not send my mother and wife any money at present; I left 10 florins with my mother when I came away; she has since got 9 or 10 florins by selling works of art. Dratzieher has paid her 12 florins, and I have sent her 9 florins by Sebastian Imhof, of which she has to pay Pfinzing and Gartner 7 florins for rent. I gave my wife 12 florins and she got 13 more at Frankfort, making all together 25 florins, so I don't think she will be in any need, and if she does want anything, her brother will have to help her, until I come home, when I will repay him honourably. Herewith let me commend myself to you.

Given at Venice on the day of the Holy Three Kings (Epiphany), the year 1506. Greet for me Stephen Paumgartner and my other good friends who ask after me.

—Albrecht Dürer

7th February, 1506

First my willing service to you, dear Master. If it is well with you, I am as whole-heartedly glad as I should be for myself. I wrote to you recently. I hope the letter reached you. In the meantime my mother has written to me, chiding me for not writing to you, and has given me to understand that you are displeased with me because I do not write to you; and that I must excuse myself to you fully. And she is much worried about it, as is her wont. Now I do not know what excuse to make, except that I am lazy about writing and that you have not been at home. But as soon as I knew that you were at home or were coming home, I wrote to you at once; I also specially charged Castel (Fugger) to convey my service to you.

Therefore I most humbly beg you to forgive me, for I have no other friend on earth but you; but I do not believe you are angry with me, for I hold you as no other than a father.

How I wish you were here at Venice, there are so many good fellows among the Italians who seek my company more and more every day—which is very gratifying to me—men of sense, and scholarly, good lute-players, and pipers, connoisseurs in painting, men of much noble sentiment and honest virtue, and they show me much honour and friendship. On the other hand, there are also amongst them the most faithless, lying, thievish rascals; such as I scarcely believed could exist on earth; and yet if one did not know them, one would think that they were the nicest men on earth. I cannot help laughing to myself when they talk to me: they know that their villainy is well known, but that does not bother them.

I have many good friends among the Italians who warn me not to eat and drink with their painters, for many of them are my enemies and copy my work in the churches and wherever they can find it; afterwards they criticize it and claim that it is not done in the antique style and say it is no good, but Giambellin (Giovanni Bellini) has praised me highly to many gentlemen. He would willingly have something of mine, and came himself to me and asked me to do something for him, and said that he would pay well for it, and everyone tells me what an upright man he is, so that I am really friendly with him. He is very old and yet he is the best painter of all.

[Editor's note: The character of Bellini agrees with all we know of him. Camerarius tells an amusing story of the two artists, to the effect that Bellini once asked Dürer for one of the brushes with which he painted hairs. Dürer produced several quite ordinary brushes and offered them to Bellini. Bellini replied that he did not mean those, but some brush with the hairs divided which would enable him to draw a number of fine parallel lines such as Dürer did. Dürer assured him that he used no special kind, and proceeded to draw a number of long wavy lines like tresses with such absolute regularity and parallelism that Bellini declared that nothing but seeing it done would have convinced him that such a feat of skill was possible.]

And the thing which pleased me so well eleven years ago pleases me no longer, and if I had not seen it myself, I would not have believed anyone who told me. And you must know too that there are many better painters here than Master Jacob (Jacopo de Barbari), though Antonio Kolb would take an oath that there was no better painter on earth than Jacob. Others sneer at him and say if he were any good, he would stay here. I have only today begun the sketch of my picture, for my hands are so scabby that I could not work, but I have cured them.

And now be lenient with me and do not get angry so quickly, but be gentile like me. You will not learn from me, I do not know why. My dear, I should like to know whether any of your loves is dead—that one close by the water, for instance, or the one like [drawing of a flower] or [drawing of a brush] or [drawing of a running dog]'s girl so that you might get another in her stead.

Given at Venice at the ninth hour of the night on Saturday after Candlemas in the year 1506. [Editor's note: Reckoning from sunset, at this season [this] would be about 2:30 a.m.] Give my service to Stephen Paumgartner and to Masters Hans Harsdorfer and Volkamer.

—Albrecht Dürer

28th February, 1506

First my willing service to you, dear Herr Pirkheimer. If things go well with you, then I am indeed glad. Know, too, that by the grace of God I am doing well and working fast. Still I do not expect to have finished before Whitsuntide. I have sold all my pictures except one. For two I got 24 ducats, and the other three I gave for these three rings, which were valued in the exchange as worth 24 ducats, but I have shown them to some good friends and they say they are only worth 22, and as you wrote to me to buy you some jewels, I thought that I would send you the rings by Franz Imhof. Show them to people who understand them, and if you like them, keep them for what they are worth. In case you do not want them, send them back by the next messenger, for here at Venice a man who helped to make the exchange will give me 12 ducats for the emerald and 10 ducats for the ruby and diamond, so that I need not lose more than 2 ducats.

I wish you had occasion to come here, I know the time would pass quickly, for there are so many nice men here, real artists. And I have such a crowd of foreigners (Italians) about me that I am forced sometimes to shut myself up, and the gentlemen all wish me well, but few of the painters.

Dear Master, Andreas Kunhofer sends you his service and means to write to you by the next courier. Herewith let me be commended to you, and I also commend my mother to you. I am wondering greatly why she has not written to me for so long, and as for my wife, I begin to think that I have lost her, and I am surprised too that you do not write to me, but I have read the letter which you wrote to Sebastian Imhof about me. Please give the two enclosed letters to my mother, and have patience, I pray, till God brings me home, when I will honourably repay you. My greetings to Stephen Pirkheimer and other good friends, and let me know if any of your loves are dead. Read this according to the sense: I am hurried.

Given in Venice, the Sunday before Whitsunday, the year 1506.

—Albrecht Dürer

[p.s.] Tomorrow it is good to confess.

8th March, 1506

First my willing service to you, dear Herr Pirkheimer. I send you herewith a ring with a sapphire about which you wrote so urgently. I could not send it sooner, for the past two days I have been running around to all the German and Italian goldsmiths that are in all Venice with a good assistant whom I hired: and we made comparisons, but were unable to match this one at the price, and only after much entreaty could I get it for 18 ducats 4 marcelli from a man who was wearing it on his own hand and who let me have it as a favour, as I gave him to understand that I wanted it for myself. And as soon as I had bought it a German goldsmith wanted to give me 3 ducats more for it than I paid, so I hope that you will like it. Everybody says that it is a good stone, and that in Germany it would be worth about 50 florins; however, you will know whether they tell truth or lies. I understand nothing about it. I had first of all bought an amethyst for 12 ducats from a man whom I thought was a good friend, but he deceived me, for it was not worth 7; but the matter was arranged between us by some good fellows: I will give him back the stone and make him a present of a dish of fish. I was glad to do so and took my money back quickly. As my good friend values the ring, the stone is not worth much more than 10 Rhenish florins, whilst the gold of the ring weighs about up to 5 florins, so that I have not gone beyond the limit set me, as you wrote "from 15 to 20 florins." But the other stone I have not yet been able to buy, for 10 one finds them rarely in pairs; but I will do all I can about it. They say here that such trumpery fool's work is to be had cheaper in Germany, especially now at the Frankfurt Fair. For the Italians take such stuff abroad, and they laugh at me, especially about the jacinth cross, when I speak of 2 ducats, so write quickly and tell me what I am to do. I have heard of a good diamond ornament in a certain place, but I do not yet know what it will cost. I shall buy it for you until you write again, for emeralds are as dear as anything I have seen in all my days. It is easy enough for anyone to get a small amethyst if he thinks it worth 20 or 25 ducats.

It really seems to me you must have taken a mistress; only beware you don't get a master. But you are wise enough about your own affairs.

Dear Pirkheimer, Andreas Kunhofer sends you his service. He intends in the meantime to write to you, and he prays you if necessary to explain for him to the Council why he does not stay at Padua; he says there is nothing there for him to learn. Don't be angry I pray you with me for not sending all the stones on this occasion, for I could not get them all ready. My friends tell me that you should have the stone set with a new foil and it will look twice as good again, for the ring is old, and the foil spoiled. And I beg you too to tell my mother to write me soon and have good care of herself. Herewith I commend myself to you.

Given at Venice on the second Sunday in Lent, 1506.

—Albrecht Dürer

[p.s.] Greetings to your loves.

2nd April, 1506

First my willing service to you, dear Sir.

I received a letter from you on the Thursday before Palm Sunday, together with the emerald ring, and went immediately to the man from whom I got the rings. He will give me back my money for it, although it is a thing that he does not like to do; however, he has given me his word and he must hold to that. Do you know that the jewelers buy emeralds abroad and sell them here at a profit? But my friends tell me that the other two rings are well worth 6 ducats apiece, for they say that they are fine and clear and contain no flaws. And they say that instead of taking them to the valuer you should enquire for such rings as they can show you and then compare them and see whether they are like them; and if when I got them by exchange I had been willing to lose 2 ducats on the three rings, Bernard Holzbeck, who was present at the transaction, would have bought them of me. I have since sent you a sapphire ring by Franz Imhof, I hope it has reached you. I think I made a good bargain at that place, for they offered to buy it of me at a profit on the spot. But I shall find out from you, for you know that I understand nothing about such things and am forced to trust those who advise me.

The painters here you must know are very unfriendly to me. They have summoned me three times before the magistrates, and I have had to pay 4 florins to their School. You must know too that I might have gained much money if I had not undertaken to make the painting for the Germans, for there is a great deal of work in it and I cannot well finish it before Whitsuntide; yet they only pay me 85 ducats for it. [Editor's note: Bellini at this time received 100 ducats for a large picture]. That, you know, will go in living expenses, and then I have bought some things, and have sent some money away, so that I have not much in hand now; but I have made up my mind not to leave here until God enables me to repay you with thanks and to have too florins over besides. I should easily earn this if I had not got to do the German picture, for, except the painters, everyone wishes me well.

Please tell my mother to speak to Wolgemut about my brother, and to ask him whether he can give him work until I get back, or whether he can find employment with others. [Editor's note: Dürer's brother was Hans Dürer, who was fifteen at this date. He became a painter of second-rate ability, and afterwards helped Albrecht in the decoration of the Emperor Maximilian's prayer book]. I should like to have brought him with me to Venice, which would have been useful both to me and to him and he would have learned the language, but she was afraid that the sky would fall on him. I pray you keep an eye on him: women are no use for that. Tell the boy, as you can so well, to be studious and independent till I come, and not to rely on his mother, for I cannot do everything although I shall do my best. If it were only for myself, I should not starve; but to provide for so many is too hard for me, and nobody is throwing money away.

Now I commend myself to you, and tell my mother to be ready to sell at the Crown Fair. I am expecting my wife to come home, and have written to her too about everything. I shall not purchase the diamond ornament until you write. I do not think I shall be able to return home before next Autumn. What I earn for the picture which was to have been ready by Whitsuntide will all be gone in living expenses and payments. But what I gain afterwards I hope to save. If you think it right, say nothing of this and I shall keep putting it off from day to day and writing as though I was just coming. Indeed I am quite irresolute; I do not know myself what I shall do.

Write to me again soon.

Given on Thursday before Palm Sunday in the year 1506.

—Albrecht Dürer

[p.s.] Your servant

23rd April, 1506

First my willing service to you, dear Sir. I wonder why you do not write to me to say how you like the sapphire ring which Hans Imhof has sent you by the messenger Schon from Augsburg. I do not know whether it has reached you or not. I have been to Hans Imhof and enquired, and he says that he knows no reason why it should not have reached you, and there is a letter with it which I wrote to you, and the stone is done up in a sealed packet and has the same size as is drawn here, for 1 drew it in my note-book. I managed to get it only after hard bargaining. The stone is clear and fine, and my friends say it is very good for the money I gave for it. It weighs about 3 florins Rhenish, and I gave for it 18 ducats and 4 marzelle, and if it should be lost I should be half mad, for it has been valued at quite twice what I gave for it. There were people who would have given me more for it the moment I had bought it. So, dear Herr Pirkheimer, tell Hans Imhof to enquire of the messenger what he has done with the letter and packet. The messenger was sent off by Hans Imhof the younger on the 11th March.

Now may God keep you, and let me commend my mother to you. Tell her to take my brother to Wolgemut that he may work and not be idle.

Ever your servant.

Read by the sense. I am in a hurry, for I have seven letters to write, part written. I am sorry for Herr Lorenz. Greet him and Stephen Paumgartner.

Given at Venice in the year 1506, on St. Mark's Day.

Write me an answer soon, for I shall have no rest till I hear. Andreas Kunhofer is deadly ill as I have just heard.

—Albrecht Dürer

28th August, 1506

To the first greatest man in the world; your servant and slave, Albert Dürer, sends salutation to his magnificent Master Wilibaldo Pirkamer. By my faith, I hear gladly and with great pleasure of your health and great honour, and I marvel how it is possible for a man like you to stand against so many, tyrants, bullies, and soldiers. Not otherwise than by the grace of God. When I read your letter about this strange abuse it gave me great fright; I thought it was a serious matter. But I warrant you frighten even Schott's men, for you look wild enough, especially on holy days with your skipping gait! But it is very improper for such a soldier to smear himself with civet. You want to be a regular silk tail, and you think that if only you manage to please the girls, it is all right. If you were only as taking a fellow as I am, I should not be so provoked. You have so many loves that it would take you a month and more to visit each.

However, let me thank you for having arranged my affairs so satisfactorily with my wife. I know there is no lack of wisdom in you. If only you were as gentle as I am, you would have all the virtues. Thank you, too, for everything you are doing for me, if only you would not bother me about the rings. If they do not please you, break off their heads and throw them in the privy, as Peter Weisweber says.

What do you mean by setting me to such dirty work, I have become a gentiluomo at Venice. I have heard that you can make lovely rhymes; you would be a find for our fiddlers here. They play so beautifully that they weep over their own music. Would God that our Rechenmeister girl could hear them, she would cry too. At your command I will again lay aside my anger and behave even better than usual.

But I cannot get away from here in two months, for I have not enough money yet to start myself off, as I have written to you before; and so I pray you if my mother comes to you for a loan, let her have 10 florins till God helps me out. Then I will scrupulously repay you the whole.

With this I am sending you the glass things by the messenger. And as for the two carpets, Anthon Kolb will help me to buy the most beautiful, the broadest, and the cheapest. As soon as I have them I'll give them to Imhof the younger to pack off to you. I shall also look after the crane's feathers. I have not been able to find any as yet. But of swan's feathers for writing with there are plenty. How would it do if you stuck them on your hats in the meantime?

A book printer of whom I enquired tells me that he knows of no Greek books that have been brought out recently, but any that he comes across he will acquaint me with that I may write to you about them.

And please inform me what sort of paper you want me to buy, for I know of no finer quality than we get at home.

As to the Historical pieces, I see nothing extraordinary in what the Italians make that would be especially useful for your work. It is always the same thing. You yourself know more than they paint. I have sent you a letter recently by the messenger Kannengiesser. Also I should like to know how you are managing with Kunz Imhof.

Herewith let me commend myself to you. Give my willing service to our prior. Tell him to pray God for me that I may be protected, and especially from the French sickness, for there is nothing I fear more now and nearly everyone has it. Many men are quite eaten up and die of it. And greet Stephen Paumgartner and Herr Lorenz and those who kindly ask after me.

Given at Venice on the 18th August, 1506

—Albrecht Dürer

Noricus civis

P.S. Lest I forget, Andreas is here and sends you his service. He is not yet strong, and is in want of money. His long illness and debts have eaten up everything he had. I have myself lent him 8 ducats, but don't tell anyone, in case it should come back to him. He might think I told you in bad faith. You must know, too, that he behaves himself so honourably that everyone wishes him well. I have a mind, if the King comes to Italy, to go with him to Rome.

8th September, 1506

Most learned, approved, wise, master of many languages, keen to detect all uttered lies, and quick to recognize real truth, honourable,

Herr Wilibald Pirkheimer, your humble servant, Albrecht Dürer, wishes you all health, great and worthy honour, with the devil as much of such nonsense as you like.

I will wager that for this you too would think me an orator of a hundred headings. A chamber must have more than four corners which is to contain gods of memory. I will not addle my pate with it. I will recommend it to you, but I believe that however many chambers there may be in the head, you would have a little bit in each of them. The Margrave would not grant a long enough audience. A hundred headings and to each head say a hundred words: that takes 9 days, 7 hours, 52 minutes, not counting the sighs, which I have not yet reckoned; but you could not get through the whole in one go: it would draw itself out like some dotard's speech.

I have taken every trouble about the carpets, but I cannot find any wide ones; they are all narrow and long. However, I still look out for them every day, and so does Anthon Kolb.

I gave your respects to Bernhard Hirschvogel and he sent you his service. He is full of sorrow for the death of his son, the nicest boy that I have ever seen. I can't get any of your fool's feathers. Oh, if you were only here, how you would admire these fine Italian soldiers! How often I think of you! Would God that you and Kuntz Kamerer could see them! They have scythe-shaped lances with 218 points; if they only touch a man with them he dies, for they are all poisoned. Heigho! but I can do it well, I'll be an Italian soldier. The Venetians are collecting many men; so is the Pope and the King of France. What will come of it I don't know, for people scoff at our King a great deal.

Wish Stephen Paumgartner much happiness from me. I can't wonder at his having taken a taken wife. My greeting to Borsch, Herr Lorenz, and our fair friend, as well as to your Rechenmeister girl, and thank your Club for its greeting; says it's a dirty one. I sent you olive-wood from Venice to Augsburg, where I let it stay, a full ten hundred weight. But it says it won't wait, hence the stink.

My picture [the self-portrait Dürer painted?], you must know, says it would give a ducat for you to see it. It is well painted and finely coloured. I have got much praise but little profit by it. I could have easily earned 200 ducats in the time, and I have had to decline big commissions in order to come home.

I have shut up all the painters, who used to say that I was good at engraving, but that in painting I didn't know how to handle my colours. Now they all say they never saw better colouring.

My French mantle greets you, and so does my Italian coat. It seems to me that you smell of gallantry. I can scent it from here; and they say here, that when you go courting, you pretend to be no more than 25 years old. Oh, yes! Multiply that and I`ll believe it. My friend, there `s a devil of a lot of Italians here who are just like you. I don't know how it is!

The Doge and the Patriarch have seen my picture. Herewith let me commend myself as your servant. I really must sleep, for it's striking seven at night, and I have already written to the Prior of the Augustines, to my father-in-law, to Mistress Dietrich, and to my wife, and they are all sheets cram full. So I have had to hurry over this. Read according to the sense. You would do it better if you were writing to princes. Many good nights to you, and days too. Given at Venice on Our Lady's Day in September.

You needn't lend my wife and mother anything. They have got money enough.

—Albert Dürer

23 Sept. 1506

Your letter telling me of the overflowing praise that you received from princes and nobles gave me great allegrezza. [Editor's note: Allegrezza means "joy;" in Venetian in original]. You must have changed completely to have become so gentle; I must do likewise when I meet you again. Know also that my picture is finished, likewise another quadro, [Editor's note: quadro is Venetian for "painting"] the like of which I never made before. And as you are so pleased with yourself, let me tell you now that there is no better Madonna picture in all the land, for all the painters praise it as the nobles do you. They say that they have never seen a nobler, more charming painting.

The oil for which you wrote I am sending by Kannengiesser. And burnt glass that I sent you by Farber—tell me if it reached you safely. As for the carpets, I have not bought any yet, for I cannot find any square ones. They are all narrow and long. If you would like any of these, I will willingly buy them; let me know about it.

Know also that in four weeks at the latest I shall be finished here, for I have to paint first some portraits that I have promised, and in order that I may get home soon, I have refused, since my picture was finished, orders for more than 2,000 ducats; all my neighbours know of this.

Now let me commend myself to you. I had much more to write, but the messenger is ready to start: besides, I hope, if God will, to be with you again soon and to learn new wisdom from you. Bernhard Holzbeck told me great things of you, but I believe that he did so because you have become his brother- in-law. But nothing makes me more angry than to hear anyone say that you are handsome, for then I should have to be ugly; that would make me mad.

The other day I found a gray hair on my head, which was produced by sheer misery and annoyance. I think I am fated to have evil days. My French mantle and the doublet and the brown coat send you a hearty greeting. But I should like to see what your drinking club can do that you hold yourself so high.

Given the year 1506 on Wednesday after St. Matthew's

—Albrecht Dürer

About the 13th October, 1506

Once I know that you are aware of my devotion to your service, there is no need to write about it; but so much the more necessary is it for me to tell you of the great delight it gives me to hear of the high honour and fame that you have attained to by your manly wisdom and learned skill. This is the more to be wondered at, for seldom or never can the like be found in a young body; but it comes to you by the special grace of God, as it does to me. How pleased we both feel when we think well of ourselves, I with my picture, and you con vostra [with your] learning! When anyone praises us we hold up our head and believe him, yet perhaps he is only some false flatterer who is making fun of us, so don't credit anyone who praises you, for you have no notion how unmannerly you are.

I can readily portray you to myself standing before the Margrave and making pretty speeches. You carry on just as though you were making love to the Rosentaler girl, cringing so.

It did not escape me, when you wrote the last letter, you were full of amorous thoughts. You ought to be ashamed of yourself, for making yourself out so good looking when you are so old. Your flirting is like a big shaggy dog playing with a little kitten. If you were only as nice and sleek as I am, I might understand it; but when I get to be a burgomaster I will shame you with the Luginsland [Editor's note: this was a Nuremberg prison], as you do the pious Zamener and me. I will have you shut up there for once with the Rechenmeister, Rosentaler, Gartner, Schlitz, and Por girls, and many others whom for shortness I will not name. They must deal with you. They ask after me more than after you, however, for you yourself write that both girls and ladies ask after me—that is a sign of my virtue! But if God brings me home again safely, I do not know how I shall get along with you with your great wisdom: but I `m glad on account of your virtue and good nature; and your dogs will be the better for it, for you will not beat them lame any more. But if you are so highly respected at home, you will not dare to be seen speaking with a poor painter in the streets, it would be a great disgrace, con poltrone di pintore.

Oh, dear Herr Pirkheimer, this very minute, while I was writing to you in good humour, the fire alarm sounded and six houses over by Peter Pender's are burned, and woolen cloth of mine, for which I paid only yesterday 8 ducats, is burned; so I too am in trouble. There are often fire alarms here.

As for your plea that I should come home quickly, I will come just as soon as I can; but I must first gain money for my expenses. I have paid out about 100 ducats for colours and other things, and I have ordered two carpets which I shall pay for tomorrow; but I could not get them cheaply. I will pack them up with my linen.

As for your previous comment that I should come home soon or else you would give my wife a "washing," you are not permitted to do so, since you would ride her to death.

Know, too, that I decided to learn dancing and went twice to the school, for which I had to pay the master a ducat. No one could get me to go there again. To learn dancing, I should have had to pay away all that I have earned, and at the end I should have known nothing about it.

As for the glass, the messenger Farber will bring it to you. I cannot find out anywhere that they are printing any new Greek books. I will pack up a ream of your paper for you. I thought Keppler had more like it; but I have not been able to get the feathers you wanted, and so I bought white ones instead. If I find the green ones, I will buy some and bring them with me.

Stephen Paumgartner has written to me to buy him fifty Carnelian beads for a rosary. I have ordered them, but they are dear. I could not get any larger ones, and shall send them to him by the next messenger.

As to your question as to when I shall come home, I tell you, so that my lords may make their arrangements, that I shall have finished here in ten days. After that I should like to travel to Bologna to learn the secrets of the art of perspective, which a man there is willing to teach me. I should stay there about eight or ten days and then come back to Venice; after that I should come with the next messenger.

How I shall freeze after this sun! Here I am a gentleman, at home a parasite. Let me know how old Dame Kormer behaves as a bride, and that you will not grudge her to me. There are many things about which I should like to write to you, but I shall soon be with you.

Given at Venice about the 14th day after Michaelmas, 1506.

—Albrecht Dürer

P.S. When will you let me know whether any of your children have died? You also wrote me once that Joseph Rummel had married — —z's daughter, and forgot to mention whose. How should I know what you mean? If I only had my cloth back! I am afraid my mantle has been burned too. That would drive me crazy. I seem doomed to bad luck; not more than three weeks ago a man ran away who owed me 8 ducats.

PART II: DIARY OF A JOURNEY THE NETHERLANDS (July, 1520- July, 1521)

Anno 1520

On Thursday after St. Kilian's Day, I, Albrecht Dürer, at my own charges and costs, took myself and my wife from Nuremberg away to the Netherlands, and the same day, after we had passed through Eriangen, we put up for the night at Baiersdorff, and spent there 3 crowns, less 6 pfennigs. From thence on the next day, Friday, we came to Forchheim, and there paid for the conveying thence on the journey to Bamberg 22 pf., and presented to the Bishop a painted Virgin and a "Life of the Virgin," an "Apocalypse," and a florin's worth of engravings. He invited me to be his guest, gave me a toll-pass and three letters of introduction, and settled my bill at the inn, where I had spent about a florin. I paid 6 florins in gold to the boatmen who took me from Bamberg to Frankfurt. Master Lucas Benedict and Hans the painter sent me a present of wine. Spent 4 pf. for bread and 13 pf. as tips.

Then I journeyed from Bamberg to Eltman and showed my pass, and they let me go free. And from there we passed by Zeil; in the meantime I spent 21 pf. Next I came to Hassfurt, and showed my pass, and they let me go without paying duty; I paid 1 florin to the Bishop of Bamberg's chancery. Next I came to Theres to the monastery, and I showed my pass, and they also let me go free; then we journeyed to Lower Euerheim. There I stayed the night and spent I pf. Thence we went to Meinberg, and I showed my papers and was allowed to pass. Then we came to Schweinfurt, where Dr. George Rebart invited me, and he gave us wine in the boat: they let me also pass free. 10 pf. for a roast fowl, 18 pf. in the kitchen and to the boy. Then we traveled to Volkach and I showed my pass, and we went on and came to Schwarzach, and there we stopped the night and spent 22 pf., and on Monday we were up early and went toward Tettelbach and came to Kitzingen, and I showed my letter, and they let me go on, and I spent 37 pf. After that we went past Sulzfeld to Marktbreit, and I showed my letter and they let me through, and we traveled by Frickenhausen to Ochsenfurth, where I showed my pass and they let me go free: and we came to Eibelstadt, and from that to Haidingsfeldt, and thence to Wurzburg; there I showed my pass and they let me go free. Thence we journeyed to Erlabrunn and stopped the night there, and I spent 22 pf. From that we journeyed on past Retzbath and Zellingen and came to Karlstadt; here I showed my pass and they let me go on. Thence I traveled to Gmunden, and there we breakfasted and spent 22 pf. I also showed my pass, and they let me go free. We traveled thence to Hofstetten; I showed my pass, and they let me through. We came next to Lohr, where I showed my pass and passed on; from there we came to Neustadt and showed our letter, and they let us travel on; also I paid 10 pf. for wine and crabs. From there we came to Rothenfels, and I showed my pass, and they let me go free, and we stayed there for a night, and spent 20 pf.; and on Wednesday early we started and passed by St. Eucharius and came to Heidenfeld, and thence to Triefenstein; from there we came to Homburg, where I showed my pass and they let me through; from there we came to Wertheim, and I showed my letter, and they let me go free, and I spent 57 pf. From there we went to Prozelten; here I showed my pass, and they let me through. Next we went on past Freudenberg, where I showed my letter once more, and they let me through; from there we came to Miltenberg and stayed there over night, and I also showed my pass and they let me go, and I spent 61 pf.; from there we came to Klingenberg. I showed my pass and they let me through; and we came to Worth and from there passed Obernburg to Aschaffenburg; here I presented my pass and they let me through, and I spent 52 pf.; from there we journeyed on to Selgenstadt; from there to Steinheim, where I showed my letter and they let me go on, and we stayed with Johannes for the night, who showed us the town and was very friendly to us; there I spent 16 pf., and so early on Friday morning we traveled to Kesselstadt, where I showed my pass and they let me go on; from there we came to Frankfurt, and I showed my pass again, and they let me through, and I spent 6 white pf. and one thaler and a half, and I gave the boy 2 white pf. Herr Jacob Heller gave me some wine at the inn. I bargained to be taken with my goods from Frankfurt to Mainz for 1 florin and 2 white pf., and I also gave the lad 5 Frankfurt thaler, and for the night we spent 8 white pf. On Sunday I traveled by the early boat from Frankfurt to Mainz, and midway there we came to Hochst, where I showed my pass and they let me go on; I spent 8 Frankfurt pf. there. From there we journeyed to Mainz; I have also paid I white pf. for landing my things, besides 14 Frankfurt thaler to the boatmen and 18 pf. for a girdle; and I took passage in the Cologne boat for myself and my things for 3 florins, and at Mainz also I spent 17 white pf. Peter Goldschmidt, the warden there, gave me two bottles of wine. Veit Varnbuler invited me, but his host would take no payment from him, insisting on being my host himself; they showed me much honour.

So I started from Mainz, where the Main flows into the Rhine, and it was the Monday after Mary Magdalen's Day, and I paid 10 thaler for meat and bread, and for eggs and pears 9 thaler. Here, too, Leonhard Goldschmidt gave me wine and fowls in the boat to cook on the way to Cologne. Master Jobst's brother likewise gave me a bottle of wine, and the painters gave me two bottles of wine in the boat. From there we came to Elfeld, where I showed my letter and they took no toll; from there we came to Rudesheim and I gave 2 white pf. for loading the boat; then we came to Ehrenfels, and there I showed my letter, but I had to give two gold florins; if, however, I were to bring them a free pass within two months, the customs officer would give me back the 2 gold florins. From there we came to Bacharach, and there I had to promise in writing that I would either bring them a free pass in two months, or pay the toll; from there we came to Caub, and there again I showed my pass, but it would carry me no further, and I had to promise in writing as before; there I spent 11 thaler. Next we came to St. Goar, and here I showed my pass, and the customs officer asked me how they had treated me elsewhere, so I said I would pay him nothing; I gave 2 white pf. to the messenger. From there we came to Boppard, and I showed my pass to the Trier customhouse officer, and they let me go through, only I had to certify in writing under my seal that I carried no common merchandise, and then the man let me go willingly.

From there we came to Lahnstein, and I showed my pass, and the customs officer let me go through, but he asked me that I should speak for him to my most gracious Lord of Mainz, and he gave me a can of wine, too, for he knew my wife well and he was glad to see me. From there we came to Engers, which is in the Trier territory; I presented my pass and they let me go through; I said, too, that I would mention it to my Lord of Bamberg. From there we came to Andernach, and I showed my pass, and they let me go through; and I spent there 7 thaler and 4 thaler more; then on St. James's Day early I traveled from Andernach to Linz; from there we went to the custom house at Bonn, and there again they let me go through; from there we came to Cologne, and in the boat I spent 9 white pf. and I more, and 4 pf. for fruit. At Cologne I spent 7 white pf. for unloading, to the boatmen 14 thaler, and to Nicolas, my cousin, I made a present of my black fur-lined coat edged with velvet, and to his wife I gave a florin; also at Cologne Fugger gave me wine: Johann Grosserpecker also gave me wine, and my cousin Nicolas gave me wine. They gave us also a collation at the Barefoot Convent, and one of the monks gave me a handkerchief; moreover, Herr Johann Grosserpecker has given me 12 measures of the best wine, and I paid 2 white pf. and 8 thaler to the boy; I have spent besides at Cologne 2 florins and 14 white pf. and 10 white pf. for packing, and 3 pf. for fruit; further, I gave I pf. at leaving, and I white pf. to the messenger.

From there we journeyed on St. Pantaleon's Day from Cologne to a village called Busdorf. We lay there over night, and spent 3 white pf.; and early on Sunday, we traveled to Rodingen, where we had breakfast and spent 2 white pf. and 3 pf. more, and again 3 pf. Thence we came to Frei-Aldenhoven, where we lay the night, and spent 3 white pf.; thence we traveled early on Monday to Frelenberg, and passed the little town of Gangelt, breakfasting at a village called Stisterseel, and spent 2 white pf. 2 thaler, further 1 white pf., and again 2 white pf. From there we journeyed to Sittard, a pretty little town, and from there to Stocken, which belongs to Liege; where we had a fine inn and stayed there over night, and spent 4 white pf. And when we had crossed over the Maas we started off early on Tuesday morning and came to Merten Lewbehen [sic]: there we had breakfast and spent 2 stivers and gave a white pf. for a young fowl. From there we traveled across the heath and came to Stosser, where we spent 2 stivers, and lay there the night: from thence on Wednesday morning early we traveled to West Meerbeck, where I paid 3 stivers for bread and wine; and we went on as far as Branthoek, where we had breakfast and spent 1 stiver; from there we traveled to Uylenberg, where we stayed the night and spent 3 stivers; from there we traveled on Thursday early to op ten Kouys, where we breakfasted and spent 2 stivers; thence we came to Antwerp.

There I sent to Jobst Planckfelt's inn, and the same evening the Fugger's factor, by name Bernhard Stecher, invited me and gave us a costly meal—my wife dined at the inn. I paid the driver for bringing us three, 3 florins in gold, and 2 stivers for carrying the goods.

On Saturday after the Feast of St. Peter in Chains, my host took me to see the burgomaster's house at Antwerp, which is newly built and large beyond measure, very well arranged with extraordinarily beautiful large rooms; a tower, splendidly ornamented; a very large garden; in short, such a noble house as I have never seen in all German lands. A very long new street has been built in his honour, and with his assistance, leading up to the house on both sides. I gave 3 stivers to the messenger, and 2 pf. for bread and 2 pf. for ink; and on Sunday, which was St. Oswald's Day, the Painters invited me to their hall with my wife and maid, where everything was of silver, and they had other costly ornaments and very costly meats; and all their wives were there too; and as I was being led to the table, everyone on both sides stood up as if they were leading some great lord. There were among them men of high position, who all showed me the greatest respect and bowed low to me, and said they would do everything in their power to serve and please me. And as I sat there in honour, there came the messenger of the Town Council of Antwerp with two servants and presented to me four cans of wine from the Magistrates of Antwerp, who told him to say that they wished thereby to show their respect for me and to assure me of their good-will; wherefore I returned them my humble thanks and offered my humble services. Thereupon came Master Peter, the town carpenter, and gave me two cans of wine with offer of his willing service; so when we had spent a long time together merrily, till late into the night, they accompanied us home with lanterns in great honour. They begged me to be assured of their good-will, and promised that in whatever I did they would help me in every way; so I thanked them, and laid down to sleep.

Also I have been in Master Quentin's house, and I have been in all the three great shooting places. [Editor's note: Quentin Matsys, the painter]. I had a very splendid dinner at Staiber's. Another time at the Portuguese factor's, whose portrait I have drawn in charcoal; I have made a portrait of my host as well; Jobst Plankfelt gave me a branch of white coral; paid 2 stivers for butter and 2 stivers to the joiner at the Painters' armoury.

Also my host took me to the Painters' workshop in the armoury at Antwerp, where they are making the triumphal arches through which King Charles is to make his entry. It is 400 bows in length and each arch is 40 feet wide: they are to be set up on both sides of the streets, beautifully arranged and two stories high, and on them they are to act the plays; and this costs to make, 4,000 florins for the joiners and painters, and the whole work is very magnificently done.

I have dined again with the Portuguese factor, and once with Alexander Imhof. Sebald Fischer bought of me at Antwerp sixteen "Small Passions" for 4 florins, thirty-two of the large books for 8 florins, also six engraved "Passions" for 3 florins, also twenty half-sheets of all kinds taken together at 1 florin to the value of 3 florins, and again 5 1/4 florins' worth of quarter-sheets,—forty-five of all kinds at 1 florin, and eight miscellaneous leaves at 1 florin; it is paid.

To my host I have sold a "Madonna" picture, painted on small canvas, for 2 florins Rhenish. I took once more the portrait of Felix the lute player. 1 stiver for pears and bread; 2 stivers to the surgeon-barber: besides I have given 14 stivers for three small panels, besides 4 stivers for laying in the white and preparing them. I have dined once with Alexander the goldsmith, and once with Felix Hungersberg; once Master Joachim has eaten with me, and his partner also once.

I have made a drawing in half colours for the Painters. I have taken 1 florin for expenses. I made Peter Wolffgang a present of four new little pieces. Master Joachim's partner has again dined with me. I gave Master Joachim 1 florin's worth of prints for lending me his apprentice and colours, and I gave his apprentice 3 crowns' worth of prints. I have sent the four new pieces to Alexander, the goldsmith. I made charcoal portraits of these Genoese by name: Tomasin

Florianus Romanus, native of Lucca, and his two brothers, named Vincentius and Gerhard, all three Bombelli.

I have dined with Tomasin so often: IIIIIIIIIII. The treasurer also gave me a "Child's Head" on linen and a weapon from Calicut, and one of the light wood reeds. Tomasin Imhof has also given me a plaited hat of elder pith.

I dined once more with the Portuguese; I also gave one of Tomasin's brothers 3 florins' worth of engravings. Herr Erasmus has given me a small Spanish mantilla and three portraits of men. Tomasin's brother gave me a pair of gloves for 3 florins' worth of engravings. I have once more made the portrait of Tomasin's brother Vincentius; and I gave Master Augustus Lombard two of the Imagines. Moreover, I made a portrait of the crooked-nosed Italian named Opitius. Also my wife and maid dined one day at Herr Tomasin's; that makes four meals.

Our Lady's Church at Antwerp is so vast that many masses may be sung there at one time without interfering one with another. The altars are richly endowed; the best musicians that can be had are employed; the Church has many devout services and much stonework, and in particular a beautiful tower. I also visited the rich Abbey of St. Michael, where are the finest galleries of stonework that I have ever seen, and a rich throne in the choir. But at Antwerp they spare no cost in such things, for they have plenty of money.

I have made a portrait of Herr Nicolas, an astronomer who lives with the King of England, and is very helpful and of great service to me in many matters. He is a German, a native of Munich. Also I have made the portrait of Tomasin's daughter, Maid Zutta by name. Hans Pfaffroth gave me a Philip's florin for taking his portrait in charcoal. I have dined once more with Tomasin. My host's brother-in-law entertained me and my wife once. I changed 2 light florins for 24 stivers for living expenses; and I gave 1 stiver for a tip to a man who let me see an altar-piece.

The Sunday after the Feast of the Assumption I saw the great procession of Our Lady's Church at Antwerp, where all the whole town was gathered together, with all the trades and professions, and each was dressed in his best according to his rank; every guild and profession had its sign by which it might be recognized. Between the companies were carried great costly gold pole-candlesticks and their long old Frankish silver trumpets; and there were many pipers and drummers in the German fashion; all were loudly and noisily blown and beaten. I saw the procession pass along the street, spread far apart so that they took up much space crossways, but close behind one another: goldsmiths, painters, stonecutters, broiderers, sculptors, joiners, carpenters, sailors, fishermen, butchers, leather workers, cloth makers, bakers, tailors, shoemakers, and all kinds of craftsmen and workmen who work for their livelihood. There were likewise shopkeepers and merchants with their assistants of all sorts. After them came the marksmen with their guns, bows, and cross-bows; then the horsemen and foot soldiers; then came a large company of the town guard; then a fine troop of very gallant men, nobly and splendidly costumed. Before them, however, went all the religious orders and the members of some foundations, very devoutly, in their respective groups. There was, too, in this procession, a great troop of widows, who support themselves by their own labour and observe special rules, all dressed from head to foot in white linen robes made expressly for the occasion, very sorrowful to behold. Among them I saw some very stately persons, the Canons of Our Lady's Church with all their clergy, scholars, and treasures. Twenty persons bore the image of the Virgin Mary and of the Lord Jesus, adorned in the richest manner, to the honour of the Lord God. The procession included many delightful things splendidly got up, for example, many wagons were drawn along with stagings of ships and other constructions. Then there came the company of the Prophets in their order, and scenes from the New Testament, such as the Annunciation, the Three Magi riding great camels, and other strange beasts, very skillfully arranged, and also how Our Lady fled into Egypt— very conducive to devotion—and many other things which for shortness I must leave out. Last of all came a great dragon, which St. Margaret and her maidens led by a girdle; she was extraordinarily beautiful. Behind her followed a St. George with his squire, a very fine cuirassier. There also rode in the procession many pretty and richly dressed boys and girls in the costumes of many lands representing various saints. This procession from beginning to end, where it passed our house, lasted more than two hours; there were so many things there that I could not write them in a book, so I let it alone.

I visited Fugger's house in Antwerp, which is newly built, with a wonderful tower, broad and high, and with a beautiful garden, and I also saw his fine stallions. Tomasin has given my wife fourteen ells of good thick arras for a mantle and three and a half ells of half satin to line it. I drew a design for a lady's forehead band for the goldsmith.

The Portuguese factor has given me a present of wine in the inn, both Portuguese and French. Signor Rodrigo of Portugal has given me a small cask full of all sorts of sweetmeats, amongst them a box of sugar candy, besides two large dishes of barley sugar, marchpane, many other kinds of sugar-work, and some sugar-canes just as they grow; I gave his servant in return 1 florin as a tip. I have again changed for my expenses a light florin for 12 stivers.

The pillars in the Convent of St. Michael of Antwerp are all made out of single blocks of a beautiful black touchstone. Herr Egidius, King Charles's warden, has taken for me from Antwerp the "St. Jerome in the Cell," the "Melancholy," and three new "Marys," the "Anthony" and the "Veronica" for the good sculptor, Master Conrad, whose like I have not seen; he serves Lady Margaret, the Emperor's daughter. Also I gave Master Figidius a "Eustace" and a "Nemesis." I owe my host 7 florins, 20 stivers, I thaler—that is, on Sunday before St. Bartholomew: for sitting room, bedroom, and bedding I am to pay him 11 florins a month.

I came to a new agreement with my host on the 20th August— on the Monday before St, Bartholomew's, I am to eat with him and pay 2 stivers for the meal, and extra for drink, but my wife and the maid can cook and eat up here.

I gave the Portuguese factor a statuette of a child: besides that, I gave him an "Adam and Eve," a "Jerome in his Cell," a "Hercules," a "Eustace," a "Melancholy," and a "Nemesis;" then of the half-sheets, three new "Virgins," the "Veronica," the "Anthony," "The Nativity," and "The Crucifixion," also the best of the quarter-sheets, eight pieces, and then the three books of the "Life of the Virgin," "The Apocalypse," and the "Great Passion," also the "Little Passion" and the "Passion" on copper, all together, 5 florins' worth. The same quantity I gave to Signor Rodrigo, the other Portuguese. Rodrigo has given my wife a small green parrot.

VISIT TO BRUSSELS

On the Sunday after St. Bartholomew's, I traveled with Herr Tomasin from Antwerp to Mechlin, where we lay for the night; there I invited Master Conrad and a painter with him to supper, and this Master Conrad is the good carver in Lady Margaret's service. From Mechlin we traveled through the small town of Vilvorde and came to Brussels on Monday at midday; I gave the messenger 3 stivers; I dined with my lords at Brussels; also once with Herr Bannisis, and I gave him a "Passion" on copper. I gave the Margrave Hansen of Brussels the letter of recommendation which my lord of Bamberg wrote for me, and I made him a present of a "Passion," engraved on copper for a remembrance.

I have also dined once more with my lords of Nuremberg. I saw in the town hall at Brussels, in the golden chamber, four paintings which the great Master Rogier did; and behind the King's palace in Brussels, the fountains, labyrinth, zoological garden. Anything more beautiful and pleasing to me, more like a paradise, I have never seen.

Erasmus is the name of the little man [Editor's note: not Erasmus of Rotterdam, but a clerk of Bannisis] who wrote out my supplication at Jacob Bannisis' house. At Brussels there is a very splendid town hall, large and covered with beautiful stonework, with a noble open tower. I have made a portrait of Master Conrad of Brussels by candlelight; he is my host. At the same time I drew Doctor Lamparter's son in charcoal, and also the hostess.

Also I have seen the things which they have brought to the King out of the new land of gold: a sun all of gold, a whole fathom broad, and a moon, too, of silver, of the same size, also two rooms full of armour, and the people there with all manner of wondrous weapons, harness, darts, wonderful shields, extraordinary clothing, beds, and all kinds of wonderful things for human use, much finer to look at than prodigies. These things are all so precious that they are valued at 100,000 gulden, and all the days of my life I have seen nothing that reaches my heart so much as these, for among them I have seen wonderfully artistic things and have admired the subtle ingenuity of men in foreign lands; indeed, I don't know how to express what I there found.

I also saw many other beautiful things at Brussels, and especially a great fish bone there, as vast as if it had been built up of square stones; it was a fathom long, very thick, weighs up to 1 cwt. (15 centner), and it has the form as is here drawn; it stood behind on the fish's head.

I have also been in the Lord of Nassau's house, which is so magnificently built and so beautifully decorated. I have again dined twice with my lords. Lady Margaret sent after me to Brussels and promised that she would speak in my behalf to King Charles, and has shown herself quite exceptionally kind to me: I sent her my engraved "Passion" and such another to her treasurer, Jan Marnix by name, and I made his portrait in charcoal. I paid 2 stivers for a buffalo ring, and also 2 stivers for opening St. Luke's picture. When I was in Herr von Nassau's house I saw in the chapel the fine painting that Master Hugo has made, and I also saw two large beautiful halls, and all the treasures in various parts of the house, and the large bed in which fifty men can lie. And I also saw the great stone which the storm cast down in the field close to Herr von Nassau. This house lies high, and there is a most beautiful view at which one cannot but wonder. And I think that in all German lands there is not the like of it.

Master Bernhard, the painter, invited me to dinner, and had prepared a meal so costly that I do not think 10 florins will pay for it. Three friends invited themselves to it to give me good company, to wit, Lady Margaret's treasurer, whose portrait I made, and the King's steward, de Metenye, and the town treasurer, Van Busleyden; I gave him a "Passion" engraved on copper, and he gave me in return a black Spanish bag worth 3 florins. And I also gave a "Passion" engraved on copper to Erasmus of Rotterdam; likewise one to Erasmus, the secretary of Bannisis. The man at Antwerp who gave me the "Child's Head" is called Lorenz Sterk. I took the portrait in charcoal of Master Bernhard, Lady Margaret's painter. I have taken Erasmus of Rotterdam's portrait once more. I gave Lorenz Sterk a sitting "St. Jerome" and the "Melancholy," and I made a portrait of my hostess's godmother. Six people whose portraits I painted at Brussels gave me nothing. I paid 3 stivers for two buffalo horns and 1 stiver for two Eulenspiegels.

So then on the Sunday after St. Giles', I traveled with Herr Tomasin to Mechlin and took leave of Herr Hans Ebner, and he would take nothing for my expenses while I was with him seven days; I paid 1 stiver on behalf of Hans Geuder; I gave 1 stiver as a tip to the host's servant; and at Mechlin I took supper with the Lady Nieuwekerke; and early on Monday I traveled from Mechlin to Antwerp.

AT ANTWERP (September 3 - October 4, 1520)

I breakfasted with the Portuguese factor, who gave me three porcelain dishes, and Rodrigo gave me some Calicut feathers. I spent 1 florin and paid my messenger 2 stivers. I bought Susanna a mantle for 2 florins, 10 stivers. My wife paid 4 florins Rhenish for a washtub, a bellows, a basin, a pair of slippers, wood for cooking, stockings, a cage for the parrot, 2 jugs, and for tips; she spent, moreover, for eating, drinking, and various necessaries, 21 stivers.

Now on Monday after St. Giles' I am back again at Jobst Planckfelter's, and have dined with him as many times as are drawn here-IIIIIIIIIIIIIIIII. I gave Nicolas, Tomasin's man, 1 stiver; I paid 5 stivers for the little frame, and 1 stiver more. My host gave me an Indian cocoanut and an old Turkish whip; then I have dined IIIIIIIIIIII more with Tomasin. The two lords of Rogendorf have invited me; I have dined once with them and made a large drawing of their coat of arms on wood, for engraving. I gave away 1 stiver; my wife changed a florin for 24 stivers; I gave 2 stivers as a tip. I have dined once in Focker's house with the young Jacob Rehlinger, and I have also dined once more with him. My wife has changed a florin for 24 stivers for expenses. I gave to Wilhelm Hauenhut, the servant of my lord Duke Frederick, the Platzgraf, an engraved "Jerome," and the two new half-sheets, the "Mary" and the "Anthony." I gave Herr Jacob Bannisis a good painting of a "Veronica" face, a "Eustace," a "Melancholy," and a sitting "Jerome," a "St. Anthony," the two new "Marys," and the new "Peasants." And I have given his secretary, Erasmus, who wrote my supplication, a sitting "Jerome," a "Melancholy," an "Anthony," the two new "Marys," and the "Peasants," and I have given him also two small "Marys," and all together what I have given is worth 7 florins, and I have given Master Marc, the goldsmith, a "Passion" on copper, and he gave me 3 florins in payment; besides this I have received 3 florins, 20 stivers, for prints. To the glazier Honigen, I have given four little engravings. I have dined with Herr Bannisis III. I paid 4 stivers for carbon and black chalk; I have given 1 florin, 8 stivers for wood, and spent 3 stivers more. I have dined with the lords of Nuremberg IIIIIIIII. Master Dietrich, the glass painter, sent me the red colour which is found in the new bricks at Antwerp. I made charcoal portrait of Jacob von Lubeck; he gave my wife a Philip's florin. I have again changed a Philip's florin for expenses.

I presented to Lady Margaret a seated "Jerome" engraved on copper. I sold a woodcut "Passion" for 12 stivers, besides an "Adam and Eve" for 4 stivers. Felix, the captain and lute- player, bought a whole set of copper-engravings and a woodcut "Passion" and an engraved "Passion," two half-sheets and two quarter-sheets, for 8 gold florins; so I gave him another set of engravings. I have taken Herr Bannisis's portrait in charcoal. Rodrigo gave me another parrot, and I gave his boy 2 stivers for a tip. I gave Johann von den Winckel, the trumpeter, a small woodcut "Passion," "St. Jerome in his Cell," and a "Melancholy." I paid 6 stivers for a pair of gloves. I paid 3 stivers for a bamboo rod, and George Schlaudersbath gave me another which cost 6 stivers.

I have dined once with Wolff Haller, who is employed by the Fuggers, when he had invited my lords of Nuremberg. I have received for works of art, 2 Philip's florins, and 6 stivers. I have again dined once with my wife; I gave 1 stiver to Hans Denes' boy for a tip. I have taken 100 stivers for works of art.

I made a charcoal portrait of Master Jacob, Lord Rogendorf's painter, and I have drawn for Lord Rogendorf his arms on wood, for which he gave me seven ells of velvet.

I dined once more with the Portuguese; I took the portrait of Master John Prost of Bruges, and he gave me 1 florin; it was done in charcoal; 23 stivers for a fur coat of rabbit- skin. I sent Hans Schwarz 2 golden florins for my picture in a letter sent through the Antwerp Fuggers to Augsburg, I gave 31 stivers for a red woolen shirt. I dined once more with Rogendorf. I gave 2 stivers for the colour which is found in the bricks; and I paid 9 stivers for an ox horn. I made a charcoal portrait of a Spaniard. I have dined once with my wife. I gave 2 stivers for a dozen little pipes; I gave 3 stivers for two little maplewood bowls, two such Felix gave my wife, and Master Jacob, the painter from Lubeck, has given my wife another; dined once with Rogendorf. I paid 1 stiver for the printed "Entry into Antwerp," showing how the King was received with a splendid triumph; the gates were beautifully decorated, and there were plays, much rejoicing, and beautiful maidens in tableaux vivants, whose like I have seldom seen. Changed 1 florin for expenses.

I have seen the bones of the great giant at Antwerp; his leg above his knee is five and a half feet long, and beyond measure heavy; so were his shoulder blades—a single one is broader than a strong man's back—and his other limbs. The man was eighteen feet high, and reigned at Antwerp and did great wonders, as is set out in an old book which belongs to the town magistrates.

Raphael of Urbino's effects have been all dispersed after his death, but one of his disciples, Tommaso of Bologna by name, a good painter, desired to see me, so he came to me and gave me a gold ring, an antique with a well-cut stone worth 5 florins, but I have been already offered twice as much for it; in return I gave him my best engravings, worth 6 florins. I bought a piece of calico for 3 stivers, I gave the messenger 1 stiver, and spent 3 stivers in company.

I presented to Lady Margaret, the Emperor's sister [Editor's note: Actually, she was his aunt], a whole set of all my works, and have drawn her two pictures on parchment with the greatest pains and care; all this I have put at 30 florins, and I have had to draw the design of the house for her physician, the doctor, according to which he intends to build one, and for drawing that I would not willingly take less than 10 florins. I have given the servant 1 stiver, and I paid 1 stiver for brick colour; I have given Herr Nicolas Ziegler a "Christ lying dead," worth 3 florins. To the Portuguese factor I gave a painting of a "Child's Head," worth 1 florin. I have given 10 stivers for a buffalo horn; I gave 1 gold florin for an elk's hoof. I have done Master Adrian's portrait in charcoal. I gave 2 stivers for the "Condemnation" and the "Dialogue," 3 stivers to the messenger;

to Master Adrian I have given 2 florins' worth of works of art; bought a piece of red chalk for 1 stiver. I have done Herr Wolff von Rogendorf in silverpoint. Gave away 3 stivers; did the portrait of a noble lady at Tomasin's house. I have given to Nicolas a "Jerome in the Cell," and two new "Marys." On Monday after St. Michael's Day, 1520, I gave to Tommaso of Bologna a whole set of prints to send for me to Rome to another painter, who will send me Raphael's work in return. I dined once with my wife; gave 3 stivers for the little tract. The Bolognese has painted my portrait, which he will take with him back to Rome. I bought an elk's foot for 20 stivers, besides I paid 2 gold florins, 4 stivers, for Herr Hans Ebner's little panel; dined out; changed a crown for expenses; dined out. Am taking 11 florins for my expenses to Aachen; have received 2 florins, 4 stivers, from Ebner; paid 9 stivers for wood; gave Meyding 20 stivers for sending my box.

I have taken the portrait of a lady of Bruges, who has given me I Philip's florin. I gave away 3 stivers as a tip; paid 2 stivers for fir cones and I for stone colour; paid 13 stivers to the furrier, 1 stiver for leather; bought two mussels for 2 stivers. In John Gabriel's house I have taken the portrait of an Italian lord, who gave me 2 gold florins. Bought a portmanteau for 2 florins, 4 stivers.

VISIT TO AACHEN

On Thursday after St. Michael's Day, I journeyed from Antwerp to Aachen, and I took 1 gulden and I noble with me; and after passing through Maestricht we came to Gulpen, and from there to Aix on Sunday; there I have spent up till now, with the fare and all, 3 florins. At Aachen I saw the well- proportioned pillars with their good capitals of green and red porphyry and granite which Carolus [Charlemagne] had brought from Rome and set up there. These are made truly according to Vitruvius's writings. At Aachen I bought an ox horn for 1 gold florin. I have taken the portraits of Herr Hans Ebner and George Schlaudersbach, and Hans Ebner's a second time. I paid 2 stivers for a fine whetstone, also 5 stivers for a bath and drinking in company; changed 1 florin for expenses. I gave the town servant who took me up into the hall 2 white pf.; spent 5 white pf. With companions, drinking and bathing; I have lost 7 stivers at play with Herr Hans Ebner at the Mirror. I have made a charcoal portrait of the young Christopher Groland, also of my host, Peter von Enden. I spent 3 stivers in company, and gave the messenger 1 stiver. I have taken the portraits of Paul Topier and Martin Pfinzing in my sketch-book.

I have seen the arm of the Emperor Henry, the shirt and girdle of Our Lady, and other holy relics. I have sketched the Church of Our Lady with its surroundings. I took Sturm's portrait. Made the portrait in charcoal of Peter von Enden's brother-in-law. Have given 10 white pf. for a large ox horn; gave 2 white pf. for a tip, and I have changed 1 florin for expenses. I have lost 3 white pf. at play, also 2 stivers; gave 2 white pf. to the messenger. 1 have given Tomasin's daughter the painted "Trinity," it is worth 4 florins; paid 1 stiver for washing. I took the portrait in charcoal of the Kopffrngrin's sister at Aachen, and another in silverpoint. Spent 3 white pf. for a bath; paid 8 white pf. for a buffalo horn; 2 white pf. for a girdle: paid I Philip's florin for a scarlet shawl; 6 pf. for paper; changed 1 florin for expenses; paid 2 white pf. for washing.

On the 23rd day of October King Charles was crowned at Aachen; there I saw all manner of lordly splendour, the like of which those who live in our parts have never seen—all, as it has been described.

I gave Mathes works of art worth 2 florins, and presented Stephen, Lady Margaret's chamberlain, with 3 prints. Paid 1 florin, 10 white pf. for a cedarwood rosary; gave 1 stiver to little Hans in the stable, and 1 stiver to the child in the house; lost 2% stivers at play; spent 2 stivers, gave 2 stivers to the barber. I have again changed 1 florin; I gave away 7 white pf. in the house on leaving.

SECOND VISIT TO COLOGNE

And I traveled from Aachen to Julich, and thence to...; paid 4 stivers for two eye-glasses. I played away 2 stivers in an embossed silver medal of the king. I have given 8 white pf. for two ox horns. On the Friday before St. Simon and St. Jude I left Aachen and traveled to Duren, where I visited the church where St. Anne's head is. Thence we traveled and came on Sunday, which was St. Simon and St. Jude's Day, to Cologne. I had lodging, food, and drink at Brussels with my lords of Nuremberg, and they would take nothing from me for it, and at Aachen likewise I ate with them three weeks and they brought me to Cologne, and would take nothing for it.

I have bought a tract of Luther's for 5 white pf. besides 1 white pf. for the "Condemnation of Luther," the pious man, besides 1 white pf. for a Paternoster, and 2 white pf. for a girdle, I white pf. for one pound of candles; changed 1 florin for expenses. I had to give Herr Leonhard Groland my great ox horn, and to Hans Ebner I had to give my large rosary of cedarwood. Paid 6 white pf. for a pair of shoes; I gave 2 white pf. for a little skull; 1 white pf. I gave for beer and bread; 1 white pf. for a "pertele" [braid]. I have given 4 white pf. to two messengers; I have given 2 white pf. to Nicolas's daughter for lace, also 1 white pf. to a messenger. I gave prints worth 2 florins to Herr Ziegler Linhard; paid the barber 2 white pf. paid 3 white pf. and then 2 white pf. for opening the picture which Master Stephan made at Cologne; I gave the messenger 1 white pf., and spent 2 white pf. drinking in company. I made the portrait of Gottschalk's sister: 1 paid I white pf. for a little tract.

At Cologne, on Sunday evening after All Saints' Day in the year 1520, I saw the nobles dance and banquet in the Emperor Charles's dancing saloon: it was splendidly arranged. I have drawn for Staiber his coat of arms on wood. I gave a "Melancholy" to a young count at Cologne, and a new "Mary" to Duke Frederick. I have made Nicolas Hailer's portrait in charcoal; paid 2 white pf. to the door porter. I have given 3 white pf. for two little tracts, also 10 white pf. for a cow horn. At Cologne I went to St. Ursula's Church and to her grave, and saw the holy maiden and the other great relics. Fernberger's portrait I took in charcoal; changed 1 florin for expenses. I gave Nicolas's wife 8 white pf. when she invited me as a guest. I bought two prints for 1 stiver. Herr Hans Ebner and Herr Nicolas Groland would take nothing from me for eight days at Brussels, three weeks at Aachen, and fourteen days at Cologne. I made the nun's portrait, and gave 7 white pf. to the nun. I made her a present of three half-sheet engravings on copper.

My Confirmation from the Emperor came to my lords of Nuremberg the Monday after St. Martin's, the year 1520, after great trouble and labour. I gave Nicolas's daughter 7 white pf. on departing, 1 florin to his wife, and again 1 ort to his daughter on leaving; and I started away from Cologne. Before that, Staiber invited me once as his guest, and so did my cousin Nicolas once, and old Wolfgang once, and once besides I dined as his guest. I have given Nicolas's man a "Eustace" on leaving, and his little daughter another ort, as they took much trouble for me. I have given 1 florin for a little ivory skull, and I white pf. for a turned box, also 7 white pf. for a pair of shoes, and I gave Nicolas's man a "Nemesis" on leaving.

SECOND JOURNEY FROM COLOGNE TO ANTWERP

I started off early by boat from Cologne on Wednesday after St. Martin's, and went as far as . . . Paid 6 white pf. for a pair of shoes. I gave 4 white pf. to the messenger. From Cologne I traveled by the Rhine to Zons, from Zons to Neuss, and from thence to Stain where we stayed the day, and I spent 6 white pf. Thence we came to Dusseldorf, a little town, where I spent 2 white pf.; from thence to Kaiserswerth; from thence to Duisburg, another little town, and we passed two castles, Angerort and Rurort; thence we went to Orsoy, a little town; from thence we went to Rheinberg, another little town, where I lay overnight, and spent 6 white pf.; from there I traveled to the following towns, Burg Wesel, Rees, and from there to Emmerich. We came next to Thomas, and from there to Nymwegen; there we stayed over the night and spent 4 white pf.; from Nymwegen I traveled to Tiel, and from there to Herzogenbusch. At Emmerich I stopped and spent 3 white pf. on a very good meal. There I took the portrait of a goldsmith's apprentice, Peter Federmacher of Antwerp, and of a woman. The reason of our staying was that a great storm of wind overtook us. I spent besides 5 white pf., and I changed 1 florin for expenses; also I took the host's portrait, and we did not get to Nymwegen until Sunday; I gave the boatmen 20 white pf. Nymwegen is a beautiful city, and has a fine church and a well-situated castle; from there we traveled to Tiel, where we left the Rhine and continued on the Maas to Heerewarden, where the two towers stand; there we lay over night, and during this day I spent 7 stivers. From there we started early on Tuesday for Bommel on the Maas; there a great storm of wind overtook us and we hired some peasant horses and rode without saddles as far as Herzogenbusch, and I paid 1 florin for the journey by boat and horse. Herzogenbusch is a beautiful city, and has an extremely beautiful church and a strong fortress; there I spent 10 stivers, although Arnold settled for the repast. The goldsmiths came to me and showed me great honour. From there we traveled on Our Lady's Day early and came through the large and beautiful village of Oosterwyck. We breakfasted at Tilborch and spent 4 white pf.; from there we came to Baarle, lay the night there, and spent 3 stivers, and my companions got into an argument with the innkeeper, so we went on in the night to Hoogstraten; there we stopped two hours and went by St. Leonhard Kirchen to Harscht. We breakfasted there and spent 4 stivers.

SECOND STAY AT ANTWERP (November 22-December 3, 1520)

From there we journeyed to Antwerp and gave the driver 15 stivers. This was on Thursday after Our Lady's Assumption [by error for Presentation]; and I gave an engraving of the "Passion" to John, Jobst Schwager's man, and I made a portrait of Nicolas Sopalis, and on the Thursday after Our Lady's Assumption [Presentation], 1520, I was once more back in Jobst Planckfelt's house; I have eaten with him IIII times. My wife-II-changed 1 florin for expenses, besides a crown; and the seven weeks that I have been away my wife and maid have spent 7 crowns and bought another 4 florins' worth of things. I spent 4 stivers in company. I have dined with Tomasin IIIIII times. On St. Martin's Day my wife had her purse cut off in Our Lady's Church at Antwerp; there were 2 florins in it, and the purse itself, besides what was in it, was worth another florin, and some keys were in it, too. On the eve before St. Catherine's I paid Jobst Planckfelt, my host, 10 gold crowns for my reckoning. I dined two times with the Portuguese. Rodrigo gave me six Indian nuts, so I gave his boy 2 stivers for a tip. I paid 19 stivers for parchment; changed 2 crowns for expenses.

I sold two "Adam and Eves," one "Sea Monster," one "Jerome," one "Knight," one "Nemesis," one "St. Eustace," one whole sheet, besides seventeen etched pieces, eight quarter- sheets, and ten wood-cuts, seven of the bad woodcuts, two books, and ten small wood "Passions," the whole for 8 florins. Also I exchanged three large books for one ounce [ell of?] camlet. I changed a Philip's florin for expenses and my wife likewise changed a florin.

At Zierikzee in Zeeland a whale has been washed ashore by a great tide and storm; it is much more than a hundred fathoms long; no one in Zeeland has ever seen one even one-third as long, and the fish cannot get off the land. The people would be glad to see it gone, for they fear the great stink, for it is so big they say it could not be cut in pieces and the oil got out of it in half a year.

Stephen Capello has given me a cedarwood rosary, in return for which I was to take and have taken his portrait. I paid 4 stivers for furnace brown and a pair of snuffers; I gave 3 stivers for paper; made a portrait of Felix, kneeling, in his book in pen and ink, and Felix gave me one hundred oysters. I gave Herr Lazarus, the great man, an engraved "Jerome" and three large books. Rodrigo sent me some wine and oysters. I paid 7 white pf. for black chalk. I have had to dinner Tomasin, Gerhard, Tomasin's daughter, her husband, the glass painter Hennick, Jobst and his wife, and Felix, which cost 2 florins. Tomasin made me a gift of four ells of gray damask for a doublet. I have changed a Philip's florin for expenses.

VISIT TO ZEELAND (December 3-14, 1520)

On St. Barbara's Eve I traveled from Antwerp to Bergen-op-Zoom; I paid 2 stivers for the horse, and I spent 1 florin 6 stivers here. At Bergen I bought my wife a thin Netherlandish head cloth, which cost 1 florin, 7 stivers, besides 6 stivers for three pairs of shoes, 1 stiver for eyeglasses, and 6 stivers for an ivory button; gave 2 stivers for a tip. I have drawn the portraits in charcoal of Jan de Has, his wife, and two daughters; and the maid and the old woman in silverpoint, in my sketch-book. I saw the Van Bergen house, which is a very large and beautiful building. Bergen is a pleasant place in summer, and two great fairs are held there yearly.

On Our Lady's Eve I started with my companions for Zeeland, and Sebastian Imhof lent me five florins; and the first night we lay at anchor in the sea; it was very cold and we had neither food nor drink. On Saturday we came to Goes, and there I drew a girl in the costume of the place. Thence we traveled to Arnemuiden, and I paid 15 stivers for expenses. We went by a sunken place, where we saw the tops of the roofs standing up above the water, and we went by the island of Wolfersdyk, and passed the little town Kortgene on another island lying near. Zeeland has seven islands, and Arnemuiden, where I lay the night, is the biggest. From there I traveled to Middelburg. There in the abbey Jan de Mabuse has made a great picture, not so good in the drawing as in the colouring. From there I went to the Veere, where ships from all lands lie. It is a very fine little town.

But at Arnemuiden, where I landed, there happened to me a great misfortune. As we were coming to land and getting out our rope, just as we were getting on shore, a great ship ran into us so hard that in the crush I let everyone get out before me, so that no one but myself, George Kotzler, two old women, the sailor, and a little boy were left in the ship. When now the other ship knocked against us and I with those mentioned was on the ship and could not get out, the strong rope broke, and at the same moment a violent storm of wind arose which forcibly drove back our ship. So we all called for help, but no one would risk himself, and the wind carried us back out to sea. Then the skipper tore his hair and cried aloud, for all his men had landed and the ship was unmanned. It was a matter of fear and danger, for there was a great wind and no more than six persons in the ship, so I spoke to the skipper that he should take heart and have hope in God, and should take thought for what was to be done. He said that if he could pull up the small sail, he would try if we could come again to land. So we all helped one another and pulled it half-way up with difficulty, and went on again towards the land. And when those on the land who had already given us up saw how we helped ourselves, they too came to our aid, and we got to land.

Middelburg is a good town; it has a very beautiful town hall with a fine tower. There is much art shown in all things here. There are very rich and beautiful stalls in the abbey, and a splendid gallery of stone and a beautiful parish church. The town is excellent for sketching. Zeeland is beautiful and wonderful to see on account of the water, for it stands higher than the land.

I have made a portrait of my host at Arnemuiden. Master Hugo, Alexander Imhof, and the Hirschvogel's servant Frederick gave me each of them an Indian nut that they had won at play, and the host gave me a sprouting bulb.

Early on Monday morning we went back to the ship and set out for the Veere and for Zierikzee; I wanted to get sight of the great fish, but the tide had carried it off again. I paid 2 florins for fare and expenses and 2 florins for a rug, 4 stivers for a fig-cheese and 3 stivers for carriage, and I lost 6 stivers at play. When we came back to Bergen I gave 10 stivers for an ivory comb.

I have taken Schnabhan's portrait, and I have also taken the portrait of my host's son-in-law, Klautz. Gave 2 florins less 5 stivers for a piece of tin; also 2 florins for a bad piece of tin. I have also taken the portrait of little Bernard of Brussels, George Kotzler, and the Frenchman from Kamrick; each of them gave me 1 florin at Bergen. Jan de Has' son-in-law gave me 1 Horn florin for his portrait, and Kerpen of Cologne also gave me a florin, and besides this I bought two bed-covers for 4 florins less 10 stivers. I have made the portrait of Nicolas, the jeweler. These are the number of times that I have dined at Bergen since I came from Zeeland: IIIIIIIII and once for 4 stivers. I paid the driver 3 stivers and spent 8 stivers, and came back to Antwerp, to Jobst Planckfelt's, on Friday after St. Lucy's, 1520, and I have dined this number of times with him: IIII. It is paid, and my wife: IIII, and that is paid.

AT ANTWERP (December, 1520 - April, 1521)

In return for the three books which I gave him, Herr Lazarus of Ravensburg has given me a big fish scale, five snail shells, four silver medals, five copper ones, two little dried fishes and a white coral, four reed arrows and another white coral. I changed 1 florin for expenses, and like-wise 1 crown. I have dined alone so many times: IIIIIIIII. The factor of Portugal has given me a brown velvet bag and a box of good electuary; I gave his boy 3 stivers for wages. I gave 1 Horn florin for two little panels, but they gave me back 6 stivers. I bought a little monkey for 4 gulden, and gave 14 stivers for five fish. I paid Jobst 10 stivers for three dinners; I gave 2 stivers for two tracts; and 2 stivers to the messenger. I gave Lazarus of Ravensburg a portrait head on panel which cost 6 stivers, and besides that I have given him eight sheets of the large copper engravings, eight of the half-sheets, an engraved "Passion," and other engravings and woodcuts, all together worth more than 4 florins. I changed a Philip's florin for expenses, and besides that a gold florin for expenses. I gave 6 stivers for a panel, and did the portrait of the servant of the Portuguese on it in charcoal, and I gave him all that for a New Year's present and 2 stivers for a tip. Changed 1 florin for expenses and gave Bernhard Stecher a whole set of prints. I bought 31 stivers' worth of wood. I have made the portraits of Gerhard Bombelli and Sebastian the procurator's daughter. I have changed 1 florin for expenses. Have spent 3 stivers besides 3 more for a meal. I have given Herr Wolff of Rogendorf a "Passion" on copper and one in woodcut. Gerhard Bombelli has given me a printed Turkish cloth, and Herr Wolff of Rogendorf gave me seven Brabant ells of velvet, so I gave his man 1 Philip's florin for a tip. Spent 3 stivers on a meal; gave 4 stivers for tips. I have drawn the new factor's portrait in charcoal. Gave 6 stivers for a panel. Have dined with the Portuguese IIIIIII times, with the treasurer 1, with Tomasin IIIIIIIII times. Gave 4 stivers for tips. With Lazarus of Ravensburg 1, Wolff of Rogendorf 1, Bernhard Stecher 1, Utz Hanolt Meyting 1, Caspar Lewenter 1. I gave 3 stivers to the man whose portrait I drew; gave the boy 2 stivers. I have given 4 florins for flax. Have taken 4 florins for prints; have changed 1 crown for expenses. Paid the furrier 4 stivers and again 2 stivers. Lost 4 stivers at play; spent 6 stivers. I have changed 1 noble for expenses; gave 18 stivers for raisins and three pairs of knives. I paid 2 florins for some meals at Jobst's. Have lost 4 stivers at play, and gave 6 stivers to the furrier. Have given Master Jacob two engraved "St. Jeromes." Lost 2 stivers at play: changed 1 crown for expenses; lost 1 stiver at play. Have given to Tomasin's three maids three pairs of knives, which cost 5 stivers. Have taken 29 stivers for prints. Rodrigo gave me a muskball just as it had been cut from the musk deer, also a 1/4 lb. of persin [a dark red paint?] and a box full of quince electuary and a big box of sugar, so I gave his boy 5 stivers for a tip.

Lost 2 stivers at play. I have done the portrait of Jobst's wife in charcoal. I have got 4 florins, 5 stivers for three small canvases. Changed 2 florins in succession for expenses. Lost 2 stivers at play.

My wife gave me 1 florin for the child, and 4 stivers in the child's bed. I have changed 1 crown for expenses; spent 4 stivers, lost 2 stivers at play, and gave 4 stivers to the messenger. Changed 1 florin for expenses.

I gave Master Dietrich, the glass painter, an "Apocalypse" and the six "Knots." Paid 40 stivers for flax. Lost 8 stivers at play. I have given the little Portuguese factor, Signor Francisco, my small canvas with the small child, that is worth 10 florins. I have given Dr. Loffen at Antwerp the four books and an engraved "Jerome," and the same to Jobst Planckfelt. I have done the arms of Staiber and another. I have made a portrait of Tomasin's son and daughter in silverpoint; also I have painted a small panel in oil of the Duke. Have got 3 stivers for engravings. Rodrigo, the Portuguese secretary, has given me two Calicut cloths, one of them is silk, and he has given me an ornamented cap and a green jug with myrobalans, and a branch of cedar tree, worth 10 florins altogether. And I gave the boy for a tip 5 stivers and 2 stivers for a brush.

I have made a drawing for a mask for the Fugger's people for masquerade, and they have given me an angel. I have changed 1 florin for expenses. Gave 8 stivers for two little powder horns. Lost 3 stivers at play. Changed an angel for expenses. I have drawn two sheets full of beautiful little masks for Tomasin. I have painted a good "Veronica" face in oils; it is worth 12 florins. I gave it to Francisco, the Portuguese factor. Since then I have painted Santa Veronica in oils; it is better than the former, and I gave it to Factor Brandan of Portugal. Francisco gave the maid 1 Philip's florin for a tip, and afterwards, because of the "Veronica," 1 florin more, but the Factor Brandan gave her 1 florin. I paid Peter 8 stivers for two cases. I changed an angel for expenses.

On Carnival Sunday early, the goldsmiths invited me to dinner, with my wife. In their assembly were many notable men. They prepared a very grand meal, and did me the greatest honour. In the evening the old bailiff of the town invited me and gave me a splendid meal, and did me great honour. Thither came many strange maskers.

I have drawn the portrait of Florent Nepotis, Lady Margaret's organist, in charcoal. On Monday night Herr Lopez invited me to the great banquet on Shrove Tuesday, which lasted till two o'clock, and was very grand. Herr Lorenz Sterk has given me a Spanish fur. And to the above-mentioned feast came many very splendid masks, especially Tomasin Bombelli.

I have won 2 florins at play. Have changed an angel for expenses: paid 14 stivers for a basket of raisins. I have made the portrait in charcoal of Bernhard von Castell, from whom I won the money. Tomasin's brother Gerhardt has given me four Brabant ells of the best black satin, and has given me three big boxes of candied citron, so I gave the maid 3 stivers for a tip. Paid 13 stivers for wood, and 2 stivers for pine kernels. I drew the procurator's daughter very carefully in silver-point.

Have changed 1 angel for expenses. I have drawn the portrait in black chalk of the good marble worker, Master Johann, who looks like Christopher Kohler; he has studied in Italy, and comes from Metz. I have changed 1 Horn florin for expenses. I have given 3 florins to Jan Turck for Italian works of art; I gave him 12 ducats' worth of works of art for one ounce of good ultramarine. I have sold a small woodcut of the "Passion" for florins. I sold two reams and four books of Schauflein's prints for 3 florins. Have given 3 florins for two ivory salt-cellars from Calicut. Have taken 2 florins for prints; have changed 1 florin for expenses. Rudiger von Gelern gave me a snail shell, together with coins of gold and silver, with an ort. I gave him in return the three large books and an engraved "Knight;" have taken 11 stivers for prints. I gave 2 Philip's florins for "SS. Peter and Paul," which I shall present to Herr Kohler's wife. Rodrigo has given me two boxes of quince Electuary and all kinds of sweetmeats, and I gave 5 stivers for a tip, Paid 16 stivers for boxes.

Lazarus of Ravensburg gave me a sugar loaf, so I gave his boy 1 stiver. Paid 6 stivers for wood. Have eaten once with the Frenchman; twice with the Hirschvogel's Fritz, and once with Master Peter, the secretary, when Erasmus of Rotterdam also dined with us. I paid 1 stiver to be allowed to go up the tower at Antwerp, which is said to be higher than that at Strasburg. From thence I saw the whole town on all sides, which was very pleasant. Paid 1 stiver for a bath. Have changed 1 angel for expenses. The Factor Brandon of Portugal has given me two large beautiful white sugar loaves, a dishful of sweetmeats, two green pots of preserves, and four ells of black satin, so I gave the servant 10 stivers for a tip.

Paid the messenger 3 stivers. I have drawn twice in the more in silverpoint the beautiful maiden for Gerhardt. Again changed an angel for expenses; took 4 florins for prints; paid 10 stivers for Rodrigo's case. Dined with the treasurer, Herr Lorenz Sterk, who gave me an ivory whistle and a very beautiful piece of porcelain, and I have given him a whole set of prints. I also gave a whole set to Herr Adrian, the Antwerp town orator. Also I changed a Philip's florin for expenses. I presented a sitting "St. Nicolas" to the largest and richest guild of merchants at Antwerp, for which they have made me a present of 3 Philip's florins. I gave Peter Egidius the old frame of the "St. Jerome" besides 4 gulden for a frame for the treasurer's likeness. Paid 11 stivers for wood. Again changed a Philip's florin for expenses. Gave 4 stivers for a bore. Gave 3 stivers for three canes. I have handed over my bale to Jacob and Andreas Hessler to take to Nuremberg, and I am to pay them 2 florins per cwt., Nuremberg weight, and they are to take it to Herr Hans Imhof, the elder, and I have paid 2 florins on it. Moreover I have done it up in a packing case. This was in the year 1521, on the Saturday before Judicz.

Also on the Saturday before Judicz, Rodrigo gave me six large Indian cocoanuts, a very fine piece of coral, and two large Portuguese florins, one of which weighs 10 ducats, and I gave the boy 15 stivers for a tip. I have bought a lode- stone for 16 stivers. I have changed an angel for expenses. Paid 6 stivers for packing. Sent Master Hugo at Brussels an engraved "Passion" and some other prints for his little porphyry stone. I have made for Tomasin a design drawn and tinted in half-colours, from which he means to have his house painted. I painted "Jerome" in oils with care and gave it to Rodrigo of Portugal, who gave Susanna a ducat for a tip. Have changed a Philip's florin for expenses and gave 10 stivers to my Father Confessor. Gave 4 stivers for the little tortoise. I have dined with Herr Gilbert, who gave me a Calicut target made of a fish skin, and two gloves as they use them for fighting. I have given Peter 2 stivers. Gave 10 stivers for the fish fins, and 3 stivers for a tip. I have made a very good portrait in hard chalk of Cornelius, the secretary of Antwerp.

I have given 3 florins, 16 stivers, for the five silk girdles which I mean to give away, besides 20 stivers for an edging [lace?]. These six edgings I have sent as presents to the wives of Kasperi Nutzel, Franz Imhof, Straub, the two Spenglers, Loffelholz, besides a good pair of gloves to each. To Pirkheimer I have sent a large cap, a very handsome buffalo horn inkstand, a silver [medal of the] Emperor, a pound of pistachios, and three sugar canes. To Kasper Ntitzel I have sent a great elk's foot, ten large fir cones with pine kernels. To Jacob Muffel I have sent a scarlet breast cloth of one ell; to Hans Imhof's child an embroidered scarlet cap and pine kernels; to Kramer's wife four ells of taffeta, worth 4 florins. To Lochinger's wife one ell of taffeta, of 1 florin's worth; to the two Spenglers, each a bag and three fine horns; to Herr Hieronimus Holzschuher, a very large horn.

Have eaten twice with the factor; dined with Master Adrian, the secretary of the town council of Antwerp, who gave me the small painted panel made by Master Joachim [de Patinir]: it is of "Lot and his Daughters." Have taken 12 florins for prints, also I have sold some of Hans Baldung Grun's works for 1 florin. Rudiger von Gelern has given me a piece of sandalwood; I gave his boy a stiver. I have painted the portrait of Bernhard of Brussels in oils; he gave me 8 florins for it, and gave my wife a crown, and Susanna a florin worth 24 stivers. I have given 3 stivers for the Swiss jug, and 2 stivers for the ship, also 3 stivers for the case and 4 stivers to the Father Confessor. I have changed an angel for expenses; have taken 4 florins, 10 stivers for works of art: paid 3 stivers for salve; gave 12 1/2 stivers for wood; changed 1 florin for expenses; have given 1 florin for 14 pieces of French wood. I gave Ambrozio Hochstutter a "Life of Our Lady," and he gave me a model of his ship. Rodrigo gave my wife a little ring which is worth more than 5 florins. Have changed 1 florin for expenses.

I have done the portrait of Factor Brandon's secretary in charcoal; I have done the portrait of his Moorish woman in silverpoint, and I have done Rodrigo's portrait on a large sheet of paper with the brush, in black and white. I have given 16 florins for a piece of camlet measuring twenty-four ells, and it cost 1 stiver to bring home. Have paid 2 stivers for gloves. I have done Lucas of Dantzic's portrait in charcoal. He gave me 1 florin for it, and a piece of sandalwood.

VISIT TO BRUGES AND GHENT (April 6-11, 1521)

On the Saturday after Easter, with Hans Luber and Master Jan Prevost, a good painter born at Bruges, I set out from Antwerp towards Bruges by way of the Scheldt and came to Beveren, a large village. From there to Vracene, also a big village; thence we passed through some villages and came to a fine large village, where the rich farmers live, and there we breakfasted. Thence we journeyed towards St. Paul's, the rich abbey, and went through Caudenborn, a fine village; thence through the large village of Kalve, and thence to Ertvelde; there we lay the night and started early on Sunday morning and came from Ertvelde to a small town. From that we went to Ecloo, which is a mighty large village; it is plastered, and has a square; there we breakfasted. Thence we went to Maldegem, and then through other villages, and came to Bruges—which is a fine noble town. I paid 21 stivers for fare and other expenses. And arriving at Bruges, Jan Prevost took me into his house to lodge, and the same night prepared a costly meal, and asked much company to meet me.

The next day Marx, the goldsmith, invited me, and gave me a costly meal and asked many to meet me; afterwards they took me to see the Emperor's house, which is large and splendid. There I saw the chapel which Roger painted, and some pictures by a great old artist. I gave the man who showed them to us 1 stiver; afterwards I bought two ivory combs for 30 stivers. Thence they took me to St. James's and let me see the splendid paintings of Roger and Hugo, who are both great masters. Afterwards I saw the alabaster Madonna in Our Lady's Church that Michelangelo of Rome made; afterwards they took me to many churches and let me see all the fine paintings, of which there is abundance there, and when I had seen the Jan [Van Eyck] and all the other things, we came at last to the Painters' Chapel, in which there are good things. Then they prepared a banquet for me, and I went thence with them to their guildhall; there were many honourable men gathered together, goldsmiths, painters, and merchants, and they made me sup with them, and they gave me presents and sought my acquaintance and did me great honour; and the two brothers Jacob and Peter Mostaert, the town councilors, gave me twelve cans of wine, and the whole assembly, more than sixty persons, accompanied me home with many torches. I also saw in their shooting gallery the great fish tub from which they eat, which is 19 feet long, 7 high, and 7 broad.

Early on Tuesday we departed, but before that, I did Jan Prevost's portrait in silverpoint, and gave his wife 10 stivers at parting. And so we traveled to Ursel; there we breakfasted. On the way there are three villages. Then we traveled towards Ghent, again through three villages, and I paid 4 stivers for the journey, and 4 stivers for expenses; and on my arrival at Ghent, there came to me the dean of the painters and brought with him the first masters in painting; they showed me great honour, received me most courteously, and commended to me their good-will and service, and supped with me. On Wednesday early they took me to the tower of St. John's, whence I looked all over the great and wonderful town, where I had just been treated as a great person. Afterwards I saw the Jan [Van Eyck's] picture, which is a very splendid, deeply studied painting, and especially the "Eve," the "Mary," and "God the Father" were extremely good.

Then I saw the lions and drew one of them in silverpoint; also I saw on the bridge, where men are beheaded, two pictures which were made as a sign that there a son had beheaded his father. Ghent is beautiful and a wonderful town; four great waters flow through it. I gave 3 stivers as a tip to the sacristan and the lions' keeper. I saw many other remarkable things in Ghent, and the painters with their dean did not forget me, but ate with me morning and evening, and paid for everything, and were very friendly. I gave away 3 stivers at the inn on leaving. Then early on Thursday I set out from Ghent and came through various villages to the inn called "The Swan," where we breakfasted; thence we passed through a beautiful village and came to Antwerp, and I paid 8 stivers for the fare.

AT ANTWERP (April 11-May 17, 1521)

I have taken 4 florins for works of art; changed one florin for expenses. Have taken the portrait of Hans Lieber of Ulm in charcoal; he wished to pay me 1 florin, but I would not take it. Gave 7 stivers for wood and 1 stiver for bringing it; changed 1 florin for expenses. In the third week after Easter a violent fever came upon me with great weakness, nausea, and headache; and before, when I was in Zeeland, a strange illness overcame me such as I never heard of from anyone, and this illness I have still. I paid 6 stivers for a case. The monk has bound two books for me for the prints which I gave him. I have given 10 florins, 8 stivers for a piece of arras for two mantles for my mother-in-law and my wife. I gave the doctor 8 stivers, and 3 stivers to the apothecary, also changed 1 florin for expenses and spent 3 stivers in company. Paid the doctor 10 stivers; again paid the doctor 6 stivers.

During my illness Rodrigo sent me many sweetmeats; I gave the boy 4 stivers for a tip. I have drawn Master Joachim [Patinir] in silverpoint, and made him besides another likeness in silverpoint. Again changed a crown for expenses, and again 1 florin for expenses. Paid the doctor 6 stivers, and 7 stivers at the apothecary's; changed 1 florin for expenses. For packing the third bale, which I sent from Antwerp to Nuremberg by a carrier called Hans Staber, I paid 13 stivers, and I paid the carrier 1 florin for it, and I agreed with him to take it from Antwerp to Nuremberg for 1 florin, I ort, per cwt., and this bale is to be taken to Herr Hans Imhof, the elder. I have paid the doctor, the apothecary, and the barber 14 stivers. I gave Master Jacob, the surgeon, 4 florins' worth of prints. I have made a portrait in charcoal of Thomas Polonius of Rome.

My camlet cloak came to twenty-one Brabant ells, which are three finger-breadths longer than the Nuremberg ells. I have also bought four black Spanish skins, which cost 3 stivers each, and they come to 34, that makes 10 florins, 2 stivers; I paid the skinner [furrier] 1 florin to make them up, then there were two ells of velvet for trimming, 5 florins; also for silk cord and thread, 34 stivers; then the tailor's wage, 30 stivers; the camlet which is in the cloak cost 14 1/2 florins, and the boy 5 stivers for a tip.

Cross Sunday after Easter; from this I start a fresh account. Again paid the doctor 6 stivers; I have gained 53 stivers for works of art, and have taken them for expenses. On Sunday before Holy Cross Week, Master Joachim [Patinir], the good landscape painter, asked me to his wedding, and showed me all honour; there I saw two beautiful plays, the first was especially pious and devout. I again paid the doctor 6 stivers, and have changed 1 florin for expenses.

On Sunday after Our Lord's Ascension, Master Dietrich, the glass painter of Antwerp, invited me and asked many other people to meet me, and especially among them Alexander, the goldsmith, a rich, stately man, and we had a splendid dinner, and they did me great honour. I have done in charcoal the portrait of Master Marx, the goldsmith, who lives at Bruges. I bought a broad cap for 36 stivers. I paid Paul Geiger 1 florin to take my little chest to Nuremberg, and 4 stivers for the letter. I have taken the portrait of Ambrosius Hochstatter in charcoal, and I dined with him: I have dined at least six times with Tomasin. I bought some wooden dishes and platters for 3 stivers. I have given the apothecary 12 stivers. I have given two books of the "Life of Our Lady," one to the foreign surgeon, the other to Marx's house servant; I also paid the doctor 8 stivers, and gave 4 stivers for cleaning an old cap. Lost 4 stivers at play; have given 2 florins for a new cap. I have changed the old cap because it was clumsy, and have given 6 stivers more for another.

Painted a portrait of the duke in oils: have made a very fine and careful portrait in oils of the treasurer, Lorenz Sterk; it was worth 25 florins. I presented it to him, and in return he gave me 20 florins, and to Susanna 1 florin for a tip. Likewise I painted the portrait of Jobst, my host, very well and carefully in oils; he has now given me [the portrait I did of him before?] and I have done his wife again and painted her portrait in oils.

On the Friday before Whitsuntide, 1521, tidings came to me at Antwerp that Martin Luther had been so treacherously taken prisoner, for he trusted the Emperor Charles's herald, who had been granted to him with the Imperial safe conduct, but as soon as the herald had brought him near Eisenach, to an unfriendly place, he said that he would not need him any more and rode away. Immediately there appeared ten knights, who treacherously carried off the pious man, who had been betrayed; a man enlightened by the Holy Ghost, a follower of Christ and of the true Christian faith, and whether he lives yet or whether they have put him to death, I know not. If he has suffered, it is for the sake of Christian truth and because he has fought with the un-Christlike papacy, which strives with its heavy load of human laws against the redemption of Christ; and if so, it is that we may be again robbed and stripped of the fruit of our blood and sweat, that the same may be shamelessly and scandalously squandered while poor and sick men must therefore die of hunger. And this is above all most grievous to me, that God perhaps will let us remain yet under their false, blind doctrine, invented and set forth by the men whom they call "Fathers," through whom the Word of God is in many places falsely expounded or not taught at all.

[Editor's note: This form of abduction was the usual idea at the time. But Luther was really taken by the order of Frederick the Wise in order to protect him].

O God of Heaven, have pity on us, O Lord Jesus Christ, pray for Thy people. Deliver us in due time, uphold in us the right and true Christian Faith. Gather together Thy far scattered sheep by Thy voice, in the Scripture called Thy godly Word. Help us that we may know this Thy voice and may follow no other deceiving call of human error, that we may not, Lord Jesus Christ, fall away from Thee. Call together again the sheep of Thy pasture, who are still in part found in the Roman Church, and with them, too, the Indians, Muscovites, Russians, and Greeks, who have been thus cut off by the oppression and pride of the pope and by false appearance of holiness.

O God, redeem thy poor folk constrained by heavy ban and edict which it no wise willingly obeys, whereby it is bound continually to sin against its conscience if it disobeys them. O God, never hast Thou so heavily burdened a people under human laws as us poor ones beneath the Roman chair, who daily long to be free Christians ransomed by Thy blood.

O Highest Heavenly Father, pour into our hearts through Thy Son Jesus Christ such a light, that we may know thereby which messenger we are to obey, so that with good conscience we may lay aside the burdens of others, and may serve Thee, Eternal Heavenly Father, with free and joyful heart.

And if we lose this man, who has written more clearly than anyone in a hundred and forty years, and to whom Thou hast given such an evangelic spirit, we pray Thee, O Heavenly Father, that Thou give again Thy spirit to another, that he may gather together anew from all parts the holy Christian Church, that we may all live again in a pure and Christian manner, so that from our good works all unbelievers, with Turks, heathens, and Calicuts, may turn themselves to us and embrace the Christian faith.

But, Lord, Thou willest, ere Thou judgest, that as Thy Son Jesus Christ was constrained to die by the hands of the priests and rise from the dead and after to ascend to heaven, that so too, in like manner, it should be with Thy follower, Martin Luther, whose life the pope compasses, with money, treacherously towards God, him, Thou wilt quicken again. And as Thou, Lord, ordainedst that Jerusalem should be destroyed, so wilt Thou also destroy this self-assumed authority of the Roman chair. O lord, give us thereafter the new beautified Jerusalem, which descends from heaven, whereof the Apocalypse writes, the holy pure gospel which is not darkened by human doctrine.

Whoever reads Martin Luther's books may see how clear and transparent his doctrine is, for he teaches the Holy Gospel. Wherefore his writings are to be held in the greatest honour, and not to be burned; unless, indeed, his opponents, who always fight against the truth, were also cast into the fire with all their opinions, they who would make gods out of men, but then only if there were printed new Lutheran books.

"O God, if Luther be dead, who will henceforth expound the Holy Gospel so clearly to us! Ah, God, what might he not have written for us in the next ten or twenty years!" Oh, all ye pious Christian men, help me to lament this God- inspired man and pray to Him that He will send us another enlightened man.

Oh, Erasmus of Rotterdam, where wilt thou stay? Dost thou see how the unjust tyranny of worldly power and the might of darkness prevail? Hear, thou knight of Christ, ride on beside the Lord Jesus; guard the truth, win the martyr's crown! Thou art already only a little old man, and I have heard thee say that thou givest thyself but two years more in which thou mayest avail to accomplish something. Lay out the same now well for the gospel and the true Christian Faith and make thyself heard, so shall the gates of hell, the Roman Chair, as Christ says, in no wise prevail against thee: and if here, like thy Master Christ, thou were to suffer shame at the hands of the liars of this time and therefore were to die a little sooner, the sooner wouldst thou come from death into life and be glorified through Christ. For if thou drinkest out of the cup whereof He drank, with Him thou shalt reign, and judge with justice those who have dealt unrighteously.

Oh, Erasmus, hold to this, that God may be thy praise, even as it is written of David, for verily thou mayest overthrow Goliath. For God stands by the Holy Christian Church, as He only upholds the Romish Church according to His Godly will [text here corrupt]. May He help us to everlasting happiness, Who is God the Father, the Son, and the Holy Ghost, one God, Amen.

Oh, ye Christian men, pray God for help, for His judgment draws near and His justice shall appear. Then shall we behold the innocent blood which the pope, priests, bishops, and monks have shed, judged and condemned.

Apocalypse: "These are the slain who lie beneath the altar of God and cry for vengeance, to whom the voice of God answers, Await the full number of the innocent slain, then will I judge."

Again changed 1 florin for expenses, and gave the doctor 8 stivers; dined twice with Rodrigo; dined with the rich canon; changed 1 florin for expenses. I had Master Conrad, the sculptor of Mechlin, as a guest on Whitsunday; paid 18 stivers for Italian prints: again 6 stivers to the doctor. For Master Joachim I have drawn four "St. Christophers" on gray paper, heightened with white.

On the last day of Whitsuntide I was at Antwerp at the great yearly horsefair; there I saw a great number of beautiful stallions ridden, and two stallions in particular were sold for 700 florins. I have taken 1 florin, 3 ort, for prints and used the money for expenses; 4 stivers to the doctor, 3 stivers for two little books. I have dined thrice with Tomasin. I have designed three dagger grips for him, and he gave me a small alabaster bowl. I have taken the portrait in charcoal of an English nobleman, who gave me 1 florin which I changed for expenses. Master Gerhardt, the miniature painter, has a daughter about eighteen years old, called Susanna, who has illuminated a little page with a Saviour, for which I gave her 1 florin. It is very wonderful that a woman's picture should be so good. Have lost 6 stivers at play. I saw the great procession at Antwerp on Holy Trinity Day. Master Conrad has given me a beautiful pair of knives, and so I gave his little old man a "Life of Our Lady" in return. I have taken the portrait in charcoal of Johann, the Brussels goldsmith, likewise his wife's. I have received 2 florins for prints, also Master Johann, the Brussels goldsmith, paid me 3 Philip's florins for what I did for him, namely, the drawing for the seal and the two portraits.

I have given the "Veronica" which I painted in oils, and the "Adam and Eve" that Franz did to Johann, the goldsmith, in return for a jacinth and an agate with a Lucrecia engraved in it. Each of us valued his portion at 14 florins. Further, I gave him a whole set of engravings for a ring and six stones; each valued his portion at 7 florins. Gave 14 stivers for two pairs of gloves; gave 2 stivers for two small boxes; changed 2 Philip's florins for expenses. I drew three "Bearing of the Cross" and two "Mount of Olives" on five half-sheets. I have taken three portraits in black and white on gray paper; also I drew in black and white on gray paper, two Netherlandish costumes. For the Englishman I have painted his arms in colours, for which he gave me 1 florin. Besides this, one way and another, I have done many drawings and other things to serve people, and for the greater part of my work I have received nothing. Andreas of Cracow paid me 1 Philip's florin for a shield and a child's head. Changed 1 florin for expenses. Have given 2 stivers for sweeping brushes. At Antwerp I saw the great procession on Corpus Christi Day, which was very splendid. Gave in the 4 stivers for a tip and 6 stivers to the doctor; changed 1 florin for expenses; 1 stiver for a box. Have dined five times with Tomasin; paid 10 stivers to the apothecary and to his wife 14 stivers for the clyster, and 15 stivers to him for the prescription. Again changed 2 Philip's florins for expenses; 6 stivers again to the doctor, and once more 10 stivers for a clyster to the apothecary's wife, and 4 stivers to the apothecary. I gave the monk who confessed my wife 8 stivers. I have given 8 florins for a whole piece of arras, and again for fourteen ells of fine arras, 8 florins: the apothecary 32 stivers for medicines; to the messenger I have given 3 stivers and the tailor 4 stivers. I have dined once with Hans Fehler, and thrice with Tomasin. Gave 10 stivers for packing.

On the Wednesday after Corpus Christi in the year 1521, I gave over my great bale at Antwerp to be sent to Nuremberg, to the carrier, by name Kunz Metz of Schlaudersdorf, and I am to pay him for carrying it to Nuremberg 1 1/2 florins for every cwt., and I paid him 1 gulden on account, and he is to hand it over to Herr Hans Imhof, the elder. I have done the portrait of young Jacob Rehlinger at Antwerp; have dined three times with Tomasin.

On the eighth day after Corpus Christi I went with my wife to Mechlin to Lady Margaret; took 5 florins with me for expenses; my wife changed 1 florin for expenses. At Mechlin I lodged with Master Heinrich, the painter, at the sign of the Golden Head. The painters and sculptors made me their guest at my inn, and did me great honour in their gathering; and I visited the Poppenreuter's, the gunmaker's house, and found wonderful things there. And I have been to Lady Margaret's, and I let her see my Kaiser, and would have presented it to her, but she disliked it so much that I took it away again. And on Friday Lady Margaret showed me all her beautiful things, and among them I saw about forty small pictures in oils, the like of which for cleanness and excellence I have never seen. And there I saw other good works by Jan [Van Eyck] and Jacopo [de' Barbari]. I asked my lady for Jacopo's little book, but she said she had promised it to her painter; then I saw many other costly things and a fine library. Master Hans Poppenreuter invited me as his guest. I have had Master Conrad twice, and his wife once, as my guests, also the chamberlain Stephen and his wife, both as guests. 27 stivers and 2 stivers for fare. I have taken in charcoal the portrait of Stephen, the chamberlain, and Master Conrad, the carver, and on Saturday I came back from Mechlin to Antwerp. My trunk started on the Saturday after Corpus Christi week. Changed 1 florin for expenses, gave the messenger 3 stivers. Dined twice with the Augustines; dined with Alexander Imhof; paid 6 stivers at the apothecary's; dined again with the Augustines.

I have drawn in charcoal Master Jacob, and had a little panel made for it, which cost 6 stivers, and gave it to him. I have done the portrait of Bernhard Stecher and his wife, and gave him a whole set of prints, and I took his wife's portrait again, and gave 6 stivers for making the little panel, all of which I gave him, and he in return gave me 10 florins.

Master Lucas, who engraves in copper, invited me as his guest. He is a little man, born at Leyden, in Holland, and was at Antwerp. I have eaten with Master Bernhard Stecher. Gave 1 1/2 stivers to the messenger; have taken 1 florin, 1 ort, for prints. I have drawn Master Lucas von Leyden in silverpoint. I have lost 1 florin; paid the doctor 6 stivers and again 6 stivers. I gave the steward of the Augustines' Convent at Antwerp a "Life of Our Lady," and 4 stivers to his man, I have given Master Jacob a copper "Passion" and a wood "Passion," and five other pieces, and 4 stivers to his man; have changed 4 florins for expenses; gave 2 Philip's florins for fourteen fish skins; made portraits in black chalk of Art Braun and his wife. I gave the goldsmith who valued the ring for me 1 florin's worth of prints; of the three rings which I took in exchange for prints, the two smaller are valued at 13 crowns, but the sapphire at 25 crowns; that makes 54 florins, 8 stivers; and what, amongst other things, the above Frenchman took was thirty-six large books, which makes 9 florins. Have given 2 stivers for a screw knife. The man with the three rings has overreached me by a half. I understood nothing in the matter. I gave 18 stivers for a red cap for my godchild; lost 12 stivers at play; drank 2 stivers, bought three fine small rubies for 11 gold florins, 1 2 stivers; changed 1 florin for expenses. Dined again with the Augustines; dined twice with Tomasin. I gave 6 stivers for thirteen porpoise-bristle brushes, and 3 stivers for six bristle brushes.

I have made a careful portrait in black chalk on a royal sheet of the great Anthony Hainault, and I have done careful portraits in black chalk of Braun and his wife on royal sheets, and I have done another one of him in silverpoint; he has given me an angel. Changed 1 florin for expenses, paid 1 florin for a pair of shoes; gave 6 stivers for an inkstand. I gave 12 stivers for a case for packing; 21 stivers for one dozen ladies' gloves; 6 stivers for a bag; 3 stivers for three bristle brushes; changed 1 florin for expenses; gave 1 stiver for a piece of fine red leather. Anthony Hainault, whose portrait I did, has given me 3 Philip's florins, and Bernhard Stecher has made me a present of a tortoise shell; I have done the portrait of his wife's niece; dined once with her husband and he gave me 2 Philip's florins; gave 1 stiver for a tip. I have given Anthony Hainault two books; received 13 stivers for prints. I have given Master Joachim the Hans Grun woodcut. I have changed 3 Philip's florins for expenses; dined twice with Bernhard Stecher; again twice with Tomasin. I have given Jobst's wife four woodcuts; gave Friedrich, Jobst's man, two large books; gave glazier Hennick's son two books. Rodrigo gave me one of the parrots which they bring from Malacca, and I gave his man 3 stivers for a tip. Again dined twice with Tomasin; have given 2 stivers for a little cage, 3 stivers for one pair of socks, and 4 stivers for eight little boards. I gave Peter two whole sheet engravings and one sheet of woodcut. Again dined twice with Tomasin; changed 1 florin for expenses. I gave Master Art, the glass painter, a "Life of Our Lady," and I gave Master Jean, the French sculptor, a whole set of prints; he gave my wife six little glasses with rose water; they are very finely made.

Bought a packing-case for 7 stivers; changed 1 florin for expenses; have given 7 stivers for a cut [leather] bag. Cornelius, the secretary, has given me Luther's "Babylonian Captivity:" in return I gave him my three big books. I gave Peter Puz, the monk, one florin's worth of prints; to the glass painter, Hennick, I gave two large books; gave 4 stivers for a piece of glazed calico; changed 1 Philip's florin for expenses. I gave 8 florins' worth of my prints for a whole set of Lucas's engravings; again changed 1 Philip's florin for expenses. I gave 8 stivers for a bag and 7 stivers for half a dozen Netherlandish cards, and 3 stivers for a small yellow post-horn. I paid 24 stivers for meat, 12 stivers for coarse cloth, and again 3 stivers for coarse cloth. Have eaten twice with Tomasin. I gave 1 stiver to Peter; gave 7 stivers for a present and 3 stivers for sacking. Rodrigo has presented me with six ells of coarse black cloth for a cape; it cost a crown an ell. Changed 2 florins for expenses; gave the tailor's man 2 stivers for a tip. I have reckoned up with Jobst and I owe him 31 florins, which I paid him. Therein were charged and deducted two portrait heads which I painted in oils, for which he gave me five pounds of borax, Netherlandish weight.

In all my doings, spendings, sales, and other dealings in the Netherlands, in all my affairs with high and low, I have suffered loss, and Lady Margaret in particular gave me nothing for what I gave her and did for her. This settlement with Jobst was made on SS. Peter and Paul's Day. I gave Rodrigo's man 7 stivers for a tip. I have given Master Hennick an engraved "Passion;" he gave me some burning pastilles. I had to pay the tailor 25 stivers for making up the cape. I have engaged a carrier to take me from Antwerp to Cologne. I am to pay him 13 light florins, each of 24 stivers, and am to pay besides the expenses for a man and a boy. Jacob Rehlinger has given me 1 ducat for his charcoal portrait. Gerhard has given me two little pots with capers and olives, for which I gave 4 stivers as a tip. Gave Rodrigo's man 1 stiver. I have given my portrait of the Emperor in exchange for a white English cloth which Jacob, Tomasin's son-in-law, gave me.

Alexander Imhof has lent me a full hundred gold florins, on the Eve of Our Lady's Crossing the Mountains, 1521. For this I have given him my sealed signature, which he will have presented to me at Nuremberg, when I will pay him back with thanks, gave 6 stivers for a pair of shoes; paid the apothecary 11 stivers, paid 3 stivers for cord. In Tomasin's kitchen I gave away a Philip's florin in leaving gifts, and I gave his maiden daughter a gold florin on leaving. I have dined thrice with him. I gave Jobst's wife a florin and 1 florin in the kitchen for leaving gifts, also I gave 2 stivers to the packers. Tomasin has given me a small jar full of the best theriac [an antidote for poison]. Changed 3 florins for expenses; gave the house servant 10 stivers on leaving; gave Peter 1 stiver; gave 2 stivers for a tip. I gave 3 stivers to Master Jacob's man; 4 stivers for sacking; gave Peter 1 stiver; gave the messenger 3 stivers.

On Our Lady's Visitation, when I was just leaving Antwerp, the King of Denmark sent for me to come to him at once, to do his portrait; this I did in charcoal, and I did the portrait, too, of his servant Anthony, and I had to dine with the King, who showed himself very gracious to me.

I have entrusted my bale to Leonhard Tucher and given over to him my white cloth. The carrier with whom I bargained, did not take me; I fell out with him. Gerhard has given me some Italian seeds. I gave the new carrier to take home the great turtle shell, the fish shield, the long pipe, the long shield, the fish fins, and the two little casks of lemons and capers, on Our Lady's Visitation Day, 1521.

Next day we set out for Brussels on the King of Denmark's business, and I engaged a driver, to whom I gave 2 florins. I presented to the King of Denmark the best pieces of all my prints, they are worth 5 florins. Changed 2 florins for expenses; paid 1 stiver for a dish and basket. I saw, too, how the people of Antwerp wondered very much when they saw the King of Denmark, that he was such a manly, handsome man, and that he had come hither with only two companions through his enemies' country. I saw, too, how the Emperor rode forth from Brussels to meet him and received him honourably and with great pomp. Then I saw the noble costly banquet that the Emperor and Lady Margaret held next day.

Paid 2 stivers for a pair of gloves. Herr Anthony paid me 12 Horn florins, of which I gave 2 Horn florins to the painter for the little panel to paint the portrait on, and 2 Horn florins for having colours rubbed for me; the other 8 Horn florins I took for expenses.

On the Sunday before St. Margaret's Day, the King of Denmark gave a great banquet to the Emperor, Lady Margaret, and the Queen of Spain [Editor's note: probably Eleanora of Portugal, not the Spanish Queen], and invited me, and I dined there also. Paid 12 stivers for the King's frame, and I painted the King in oils—he has given me 30 florins. [Editor's note: this painting no longer exists].

I gave 2 stivers to the young man called Bartholomew, who rubbed the colours for me; I bought a little glass jar which once belonged to the King for 2 stivers. Paid 2 stivers for a tip; gave 2 stivers for the engraved goblets. I have given Master Jan's boy four half-sheets, and to the master- painter's boy an "Apocalypse" and four half-sheets. Thomas of Bologna has given me one or two Italian prints; I have also bought one for 1 stiver. Master Jobst, the tailor, invited me and I supped with him. I have paid for the hire of a room at Brussels for eight days, 32 stivers. I have given an engraved "Passion" to the wife of Master Jan, the goldsmith, with whom I dined three times. I gave another "Life of Our Lady" to Bartholomew, the painter's apprentice; I have dined with Herr Nicolas Ziegler, and gave 1 stiver to Master Jan's servant. Because of being unable to get a carriage, I have stayed on two days in Brussels; paid 1 stiver for a pair of socks.

On Friday morning early I started from Brussels, and I am to pay the driver 10 florins. I paid my hostess 5 stivers more for the single night. From there we rode through two villages and came to Louvain; breakfasted, and spent 13 stivers. Thence we journeyed through three villages and came to Thienen, which is a little town, and lay the night there, and I spent 9 stivers. From there, early on St. Margaret's Day, we traveled through two villages and came to a town which called St. Truyen, where they are building a large, well-designed church tower, quite new. From thence we went on past some poor houses and came to a little town, Tongeren; there we had our morning meal, and spent all together, 6 stivers. From thence we went through a village and some poor houses and came to Maestricht, where I lay the night, and spent 12 stivers, and 2 blanke besides, for watch money. Thence we journeyed early on Sunday to Aachen, where we ate and spent all together 14 stivers. Thence we traveled to Altenburg, taking six hours, because the driver did not know the way and went wrong; there we stayed for the night and spent 6 stivers. On Monday early we traveled through Julich, a town, and came to Bergheim, where we ate and drank, and spent 3 stivers. Thence we journeyed through three more villages and came to Cologne.

****